Praise for Richard Lederer

Richard Lederer has done it again—another delightful, witty, and hugely absorbing celebration of the English language. Is there no stopping this man?
—Bill Bryson, author of *The Mother Tongue*

Richard Lederer is to wordplay what John Philip Sousa is to marches.
—Rod L. Evans, author of *Tyrannosaurus Lex*

Richard Lederer ought to be declared a national treasure. No one has more fun with the English language.
—*Richmond Times Dispatch*

Richard Lederer is the true King of Language Comedy.
—Sidney Sheldon, author of *After the Darkness*

Thank you for reading *So That's What It Means!*, the second book in a series of two. If you crave more learning and laughter, the companion book, *A Pleasury of Word & Phrase Origins,* is available on Amazon.

Also by Richard Lederer

Adventures of a Verbivore
Amazing Words
American Trivia (with Caroline McCullagh)
American Trivia Quiz Book (with Caroline McCullagh)
Anguished English
Animal Cracker Uppers Jr. (with Jim Ertner)
The Ants Are My Friends (with Stan Kegel)
Basic Verbal Skills (with Philip Burnham)
The Big Book of Word Play Crosswords (with Gayle Dean)
The Bride of Anguished English
Building Bridge (with Bo Schambelan and Arnold Fisher)
Challenging Words for Smart People
The Circus of Words
Classic Literary Trivia
Cleverly Comical Animal Jokes (with Jim Ertner)
Comma Sense (with John Shore)
Crazy English
The Cunning Linguist
Fractured English
Get Thee to a Punnery
The Giant Book of Animal Jokes (with Jim Ertner)
The Gift of Age
Hilarious Holiday Humor (with Stan Kegel)
The Joy of Names
Lederer on Language
Literary Trivia
A Man of My Words

SO THAT'S WHAT IT MEANS!

To Betty, my fellow verbivore 5/18/22

[signature]

So That's
What It Means!

Illuminating Stories about Word Histories & Mysteries

by Richard Lederer

Author of *A Pleasury of Word & Phrase Origins*

to Dave Clary and Chip Taulbee,
who help make my columns the best that they can be

Waterside Productions

Printed in the United States of America

First Printing, 2021

ISBN-13: 978-1-956503-02-9 print edition
ISBN-13: 978-1-956503-03-6 ebook edition

Waterside Productions
2055 Oxford Ave
Cardiff, CA 92007
www.waterside.com

TABLE OF CONTENTS

INTRODUCTION

H as it ever struck you how human words are?
Like people, words are born, grow up, get married, have children, and even die. They may be very old, like *man* and *wife* and *home.* They may be very young, like *binge watching, selfie stick, emoji, hangry, gig economy, cryptocurrency,* and *EGOT,* the rare feat of winning an Emmy, Grammy, Oscar, and Tony. Or they may repose in the tomb of history, as *leechcraft,* the Anglo-Saxon word for the practice of medicine, and *murfles,* a long-defunct word for freckles or pimples.

Our lives are filled with people and words, and in both cases, we are bound to be impressed by their vast numbers and infinite variety. Some words, like *OK,* are famous all over the world. Others, like *foozle* (a bungling golf stroke) and *groak* (to stare at other people, hoping that they will offer you some of the food they are eating), are scarcely known, even at home.

There are some words that we have probably never met, such as *samara* (the pinwheels that grow on maple trees) and *ferrule* (the metal band that holds an eraser to a pencil or the metal tip of an umbrella)

There are others that are with us every day of our lives, such as *the, be, to, of,* and *and,* the five most frequently used English words.

As with people, words have all sorts of shapes, sizes, backgrounds, and personalities. They may be very large, like *pneumonoultramicroscopicsilicovolcanoconiosis,* a forty-five-letter hippopotomonstrosesquipedalian word for black lung disease. They may be very small, like *a* and *I.*

Some words are multinational in their heritage, as *remacadamize,* which is Latin, Celtic, Hebrew, and Greek in parentage. Some come of Old English stock, as *sun* and *moon* and *grass* and *goodness.* Some have a distinctly continental flavor, like *lingerie, kindergarten,* and *spaghetti.* Others are unmistakably American, like *stunt* and *baseball.*

Words like *remunerative, encomium,* and *perspicacious* are so dignified that they can intimidate us, while others, like *booze, burp,* and *blubber,* are markedly inelegant in character. Some words, like *covidiot* and *palimony,* are winkingly playful. Other words strike us as beautiful—*luminous* and *gossamer.* Some words sound rather ugly—*guzzle* and *scrod;* some sound quiet—*dawn* and dusk—and others as noisy—*thunder* and *crash.*

Words, like people, go up and down in the world. Some are born into low station and come up in the life. With the passing of time, they may acquire *prestige* (which used to mean "trickery") and *glamour* (which began life as a synonym for *grammar*). Others slide downhill in reputation, such as *homely* (which originally meant "homelike; good around the home"), *villain* ("a member of the lower class"), and *idiot* ("a private citizen").

In the year 1666, a great fire swept through London and destroyed more than half the city, including three-quarters of St. Paul's Cathedral. Sir Christopher Wren, the original designer of the cathedral and perhaps the finest architect of all time, was commissioned to rebuild the great edifice.

He began in 1675 and finished in 1710—a remarkably short time for such a task. When the magnificent edifice was completed, Queen Anne, the reigning monarch, visited the cathedral and told Wren that his work was "awful, artificial, and amusing." Sir Christopher, so the story goes, was delighted with the royal compliment, because in those days *awful* meant "full of awe, awe-inspiring," *artificial* meant "artistic," and *amusing*, from the Muses, meant "amazing."

You've just started reading a book about etymology. The etymology of the word *etymology* is the Greek root *etymon*, "true, original," and the Greek ending *-logia*, "science or study." Etymology, then, is the science or study of true and original word meanings. An etymologist is one who knows the difference between etymology, the study of word histories, and entomology, the study of insects.

About the birth and lives of words I am enthusiastic, enchanted, ecstatic, exhilarated, exuberant, ebullient, and effervescent. Ah, those wonderful words that begin with *E*: In their early lives, *enthusiastic* meant "possessed by a god," *enchanted* "singing a magic song," *ecstatic* "in a trance," *exhilarated* "made thoroughly cheerful," and *exuberant, ebullient,* and *effervescent* "overflowing, boiling over, spouting out."

Carnivores eat meat; piscivores love fish; herbivores consume plants and vegetables; verbivores devour words. I am such a creature. My whole life I have feasted on words—ogled their appetizing shapes, colors, and textures; swished them around in my mouth; lingered over their many tastes; let their juices run down my chin. Now that you have progressed this far in this Introduction, you are clearly a fellow verbivore.

Words are who we are. Words are what we do. Words inspire our hearts, spark our minds, and beget our laughter. Words move the world. Words are as great a joy as food and drink. May *So That's What It Means!* fill you with such palate-pleasing nourishment and ear-rinsing joy.

In each thematic cluster of what you're about to read, you'll see a smiley face—☺—or two. These emojis tell you that what follows will be a humorous take-off on the core subject of the cluster. I have installed these acts of comic relief to lighten up each theme and your life. I fully subscribe to this bygone but timely children's rhyme:

What's learned with pleasure
Is learned full measure.

Richard Lederer
San Diego, California
richardhlederer@gmail.com
www.verbivore.com

LAND, SEA, AIR, AND BEYOND

DOWN-TO-EARTH METAPHORS

We were once a nation of farmers, but by the turn of the twentieth century, most had moved to towns and cities. Today only two percent of Americans live on farms, and many have lost touch with our agricultural roots. In "God's Grandeur" (1877), the Jesuit poet Gerard Manley Hopkins lamented how the Industrial Age has ravaged our feeling for the land:

And all is seared with trade;
bleared, smeared with toil;
And wears man's smudge
and shares man's smell: the soil
Is bare now, nor can foot feel, being shod.

Even though our shod feet may no longer touch the soil, most Americans speak and write the metaphors that spring from the earth and those who work it. These verbal seeds lie buried so deeply in the humus of our language that we are hardly aware that they are figures of speech at all. Let's do some digging to uncover the rich, earthy agriculture from which grow so much of our speech and our writing, our thoughts and our dreaming.

Our fertile English language is cultivated by agricultural comparisons in expressions like *a vintage year, a grass roots campaign, a budding movie star, gone to seed, seedy, cut and dried, farm team, reap the benefits, mow down, separate the wheat from the chaff, cut a wide swath, crop up, feel one's oats, farm out, weed out, plow into, the grass is always greener on the other side,* and *a needle in a haystack.*

The song lyrics "This land is your land, and this land is my land" are so very true. Here, unearthed, is a bountiful crop of agricultural words and phrases:

Among the down-to-earth figures of speech that are planted in our language is the word *broadcast,* which first meant "to broadly cast seed on the ground by hand" and in 1922 took on its modern meaning with the emergence of radio.

The lines in a worried forehead resemble the grooves in the earth made by a plow. We describe such a forehead as *furrowed.*

Like well-farmed land, the fertile minds of those who read this book are carefully tended and yield a bountiful harvest. We say that such people are *cultivated.*

A harrow is a cultivating farm implement set with spikes or spring teeth that pulverize the earth by violently tearing and flipping over the topsoil. That's why we identify an emotionally lacerating experience as *harrowing.*

A mentally talented child is often identified as *precocious,* from the Latin *praecox,* "ripe before its time."

European peasants, forbidden to cut down or pick from trees, were allowed to gather wood and fruit blown down by the wind, a bounty that required little effort on the part of the lucky recipients. By extension, we today use a word that describes an unexpected stroke of good luck: *a windfall.*

Rooted in the Latin *de-,* "from," and *lira,* "furrow," is a word that metaphorically compares behavior that deviates

4

from a straight course and swerves from the conventional path in plowing: *delirious*.

In bygone days, the Old English *math* meant "mowing." Nowadays a word that means "results, effects, or consequences" is an *aftermath*.

The arduous job of hoeing long rows in uncooperative terrain gives us *a hard (or tough) row to hoe*, an expression that means "a difficult task."

Late spring frosts or pests can kill an aborning leaf or flower before it has a chance to develop. When we terminate a project in its early stages, we say that we *nip it in the bud.*

Hay is made by setting mown grass out in the sun to dry. When we want to make the most of an opportunity, we *make hay while the sun shines.*

Anyone who has ever tried to cut the tightly stretched baling wire used to bind a bale of hay knows how ornery the stuff can be. When someone or something behaves in an uncontrolled manner, we say that he, she, or it goes *haywire*.

In the word *towhead, tow* descends from an Old English word that means "flax." A towhead is a youngster—usually male, but not necessarily so—with white or pale yellow hair the color of flax. Avoid confusing *tow* with *toe*, as in this newspaper photo caption: "Linda Tinyon clutched her toe-headed son during the storm." Even worse: "Linda Tinyon clutched her two-headed son during the storm."

A popular toast rings out, *Here's mud in your eye*, which originally meant "May you find soft, rich, dark, and moist soil that will be thrown up as specks of mud as you plow it."

Much newer than these agricultural metaphors is *couch potato*, which made its debut in U.S. slang in the 1970s.

The compound compares lumpish watchers of television to lumpy potatoes: The longer couch potatoes sit, the deeper they put down their roots and the more they come to resemble potatoes. But there's more than just a vegetable image here. In *The Real McCoy,* George Hole explains: "The origins of the phrase are much cleverer than simply an image, however, since it actually relies on a pun with the word *tuber.* A potato is the tuber of a plant, while *boob tuber* was an earlier term for someone watching the *boob tube* or television."

Shaped from the pattern *of couch potato,* we now have *mouse potato, mouse* referring to the electronic mouse that helps you navigate your computer. A *mouse potato* is someone who lives a sedentary life, spending great gobs of leisure time playing computer games, surfing the net, streaming videos, and falling headlong into the screen.

An Anthology

of Flowery Words

An anthology is a collection of literary, musical or artistic works gathered in a single setting. The Greek forebear is *anthologia*: *anthos*, "flower" + *lego*, "gather" = "a gathering of flowers." Just as our land is beautified by a vast array of flowers dappling its hills, fields, gardens, and median strips, our English language is made more exquisite and colorful by an anthology of flowery words:

Because the bright yellow *cowslip* thrives in pasturelands, it shares a name with something else found in pastures—cow dung.

The English used to call a yellow-flowered weed a "lion's tooth" because the jagged, pointed leaves resembled the lion's snarly grin. During the early fourth century, the lion's-tooth plant took on a French flavor and became the *dent-de-lion,* "tooth-of-the-lion." Then it re-acquired an English accent: *dandelion.*

In Greek mythology, the blessed spent their afterlife in the Elysian fields, which were carpeted with a flower the Greeks named *asphodelos.* Over time the word gained an initial *d* and eventually became *daffodil.* LID OFF A DAFFODIL is a palindrome, a phrase that reads the same forward and backward.

Also from ancient mythology we inherit *narcissus,* a beautiful and usually white or yellow flower. The name echoes the ancient Greek myth about the doomed pair, Echo and Narcissus. One day the smashingly handsome Narcissus looked into a still forest lake and beheld his own gorgeous face in the water, although he did not know it. He at once fell in love with the beautiful image just beneath the surface, and he pined away for a love that could never be consummated. Like the narcissistic Narcissus, the flowering plant often grows on riverbanks.

Daisy was created in Old English from the poetical "day's eye." The flower is indeed a metaphor waiting to bloom, with its sunburst center, its radiating white petals, and its sensitivity to the progress of the day, opening during the sunny hours and closing in the evening and extinguishing its brightness. The poet Geoffrey Chaucer, without benefit of any linguistic manual, referred to the sun as "the day's eye, or else the eye of day." On a more macabre note, the daisy is also the focus in the slangy *pushing up the daisies*, an informal way of saying "dead and buried."

Many members of the *geranium* family exhibit long, thin, tapering fruits that resemble the beak of a bird. That's why the Greeks named the flower *geranion,* "little crane."

Iris was originally the Greek word for both "rainbow" and for the goddess of rainbows. who left a trail of color as she delivered messages. Later her name was applied to the colorful flower and to the thin, circular structure in our eyes that gives them color.

The *orchid* is not named for its elegant blossoms but for its twin bulbs, which, in the eyes of many, resemble male gonads. That's why the name of the beautiful and expensive flower is rooted in the Greek word for "testicle," *orkhis.* More than two thousand years ago, Pliny the Elder observed, "*Mirabilis est orkhis herba, sive serapias, gemina radice, testiculis simili.*" Even if you don't know Latin, I'm confident that you can deduce the meaning of the first and last parts of that statement. Pliny believed that just holding an orchid in one's hand would heighten sexual desire.

The *passionflower* was so christened not because it inspired romantic love but because parts of the flowery vine resemble the cross on which the Passion of Christ took place.

The *rose* holds a special significance in our bouquet of flowery language, which is abundant with rose idioms that often seem to be inspired by the flower's pleasant scent and beauty. *Take time to smell the roses* is to appreciate what is often ignored. If you come out *smelling like a rose,* you have emerged from a difficult situation with your reputation intact. A similar optimism perfumes *a bed of roses, everything's coming up roses, rose-colored glasses,* and *a rosy outlook.* Then there's Gertrude Stein's epiphanous "Rose is a rose is a rose."

The *tulip*'s large, cup-shaped "mouth" may remind you of "two lips," but that's not how the blossom got its name. The Dutch borrowed *tulip* from the French (*tulipan*), who purloined it from the Turks, who noted that the shape of the flower reminded them of a turban.

A garden of women's first names bloom from flowers— Acacia, Amaryllis, Blossom, Buttercup, Camellia, Cherry, Dahlia, Daisy, Danica, Flora, Gardenia, Hazel, Heather, Holly, Hyacinth, Iris, Ivy, Jasmine, Laurel, Leilani, Lily, Lotus, Magnolia, Marguerite, Marigold, Myrtle, Orchid, Pansy, Peony, Petunia, Poppy, Rhoda, Rose, Rue, Shoshana, Susannah, Veronica, Violet, Willow, Yasmin, Yolanda, and Zenobia.

While most perennials flower, they are plants, not flowers. My eighty-and-over *generation* (jocularly "a ration of genes") has been dubbed *the silent generation, senior citizens, golden agers, retirees,* and—ew!—*fuddy-duddies, duffers, old goats, geezers, coots, codgers, bags, biddies,* and *farts.* I propose the sobriquet *perennials.* As I hope this book demonstrates, we're still blooming!

OUR SEAWORTHY LANGUAGE

In "Sea Fever" (1902), the poet John Masefield penned:

> I must go down to the seas again,
> To the lonely sea and the sky,
> And all I ask is a tall ship
> And a star to steer her by.

Relatively few of us go down to the seas, and even fewer of us get to steer a tall ship. Nevertheless, we still taste the salty flavor of the nautical metaphors that ebb and flow through our language.

Consider our use of the word *ship.* We continue to ship goods, even when we ship by truck, train, or plane. We compliment someone on running a tight ship, even when that ship is an office or a classroom. And many things besides ships can be shipshape or sinking ships.

The lapping of the sea at our language is not a difficult concept to fathom. When we try to fathom an idea, we are making poetic use of an old word that originally meant "the span between two outstretched arms." Then the word came to designate "a unit of six feet used for measuring the depth of water." By poetic extension, the verb *to fathom* now means "to get to the bottom of something," and that something doesn't have to be the ocean.

11

To help you learn the ropes and get your bearings with stem-to-stern seafaring metaphors, take a turn at the helm. The coast is clear for you to take a different tack. Don't go overboard by barging ahead and rocking the boat. If you feel all washed up, on the rocks, in over your head, or sinking fast in a wave of confusion, try to batten down the hatches, clear the deck, and stay on an even keel. As your friendly anchorman, I won't rock the boat or lower the boom on you.

Now that you get my drift, consider how the following idioms of sailing and the sea wash up on the shores of our everyday vocabulary: *shape up or ship out, take the wind out of his sails, the tide has turned, a sea of faces, down the hatch, hit the deck, steer clear of, safe harbor, cruise to victory*, and *give a wide berth to.*

As attractive an explanation as it might be, *to deep six* has nothing to do with burying a body six feet deep or by walking the plank. It's a naval idiom that means "to throw overboard," with *six* signifying "six fathoms (thirty-six feet) deep." The original term came from measuring the water depth under a ship using a lead-weighted sounding line. The lines were marked at two, three, five, seven, ten, thirteen, fifteen, seventeen, and twenty fathoms. If the depth was at a mark, the leadsman would call "by the mark," followed by the number. If the depth was between two marks, he would call "by the deep" followed by the estimated number. Six fathoms would be "by the deep six." By extension, *to deep six* has come to denote generally "to get rid of someone or something."

As a barefoot boy sitting on the banks of the Mississippi River, Samuel Clemens watched stern-wheeler boats churning the muddy waters, and he heard the leadsmen sounding the depth of the river by calling out to the captains, "By the deep six ... by the mark five ... by the deep four ... by the mark three." When the river bottom was only two fathoms, or twelve feet down, he would hear the lusty cry "by the mark twain." After he left the Mississippi, and after various careers as a riverboat pilot, prospector, and printer, Sam Clemens, now a journalist, contributed an article to the *Nevada Territorial Enterprise* on February 3, 1863, and signed it with a new name—Mark Twain.

For ancient mariners, *by and large* meant "in general; for the most part." It's a nautical term in two parts. *By* means "to sail into the wind" while *large* means "to sail with the wind at your back." To say that a ship sailed well by and large meant that it sailed successfully in all conditions, passing the test with flying colors. When we say *by and large* today, we still mean "in general; for the most part" because we do not wish to sail directly into the topic. A similar sounding phrase *full and by* has a different meaning. To sail full and by is to sail into the wind, keeping the sails full of all the wind possible.

The expression *taken aback* probably conjures up in your mind an image of a person caught off guard and staggering backwards. But the origin of the phrase is nautical, too. Sailing *full and by* left an inexperienced helmsman in danger of being taken aback, which meant "to catch the wind on the wrong side of the sails." That could drive the ship backward and even break the mast.

I trust you won't be taken aback by the armada of additional salty words and seafaring metaphors:

For time immemorial a *figurehead* has been a wooden statue carved on the prow of a ship and looking down at the waves. These figures were meant to placate the gods and the sea and ensure a safe voyage. Now we think of a figurehead as someone who has the appearance of high rank but in reality holds no power.

The lee is the leeward side of the ship sheltered from the wind. Leeway is the sideways drift of a ship to the leeward side, away from the wind. Hence, when we make things easy for others, we give them *leeway,* extra space.

On sailing ships of yesteryear, the *butt* was a name for a large, lidded cask that held drinking water. These butts were equipped with "scuttles," openings through which sailors ladled out the water. Just as today's office workers gather around a water cooler to exchange chitchat and rumor, crewmen stood about the scuttled butts to trade *scuttlebutt.*

The idiom that old salts used to describe a ship in shallow water that touched bottom from time to time has been extended to designate any precarious situation or narrow escape as *touch-and-go.* A much worse predicament is one in which a ship strikes bottom and is held tight, unable to proceed. Today we use the expression *hard-and-fast* to identify any rigid rule or opinion. Similarly, like a vessel driven ashore beyond the normal high-water mark, one who is abandoned or rejected, is *left high-and-dry.*

The doldrums are those parts of the ocean near the Equator that are noted for calm winds. They pose no difficulty for fuel-driven vessels, but sailing ships can be stuck dead in the water for weeks. When we are stuck in boredom or depression, we are *in the doldrums.*

For sailors, *sheets* refer to the lines (ropes) attached to the lower corners of a sail to hold it in place. If any of the sheets came loose, the sails flapped in the wind like flags, the vessel lost power, and the crew lost control. When three sheets of on old sailing vessel broke loose, the ship would lurch, stagger, and roll from side to side like a sailor inebriated. That's why we call an unsteady state of drunkenness *three sheets to the wind*.

From the Greek word for "ship," we inherit a word that means "illness" but that originally signified "seasickness." That word is *nausea*. If you've taken a cruise and spent the first day staring at the rolling water and depositing your lunch into it, you'll appreciate the bond between *nautical* and *nausea*.

Because a mainstay is a strong rope that helps stabilize a ship's main mast, but for most of us *mainstay* means "the most important part of something; someone or something that provides primary support." In the same fleet as *mainstay* sails *flagship*, a ship that carries the commander's flag and has come to mean "the best and most important of a group."

Seafaring folk call the two posts fixed to the deck for securing the anchor line the *bitts* and a turn of rope or chain around the bitts the *bitter*. The *bitter end* refers to the final part of the anchor line near where it is fixed to the ship's bitts. When the line is paid out, sailors lowering an anchor know that only a few yards of anchor rope remain. The men have reached the end of their rope, which is just the place that this salty disquisition has reached—*the bitter end*.

CANOE

W ell, actually we're not at the end of our voyage through seafaring words and phrases. Some witty wordsmith has invented the acronym CANOE to stand for "Committee Ascribing Nautical Origins to Everything." That committee boasts thousands of members.

They claim, for example, that the expression *three square meals* originated from the Royal Navy's protocol for serving food. While the officers and captain used silver and dined off china, common seamen were issued wooden spoons to eat off square wooden plates. Such plates do exist so why not make up a plausible story that connects *square meal* with the wooden-plate artifacts? Somebody did just that, and, ever since, tour guides have perpetuated the entertaining rubbish.

Balderdash! Twaddle! Codswollop! The word *square* has many meanings, including "proper, honest, straightforward," as in *square deal* and *fair and square;* and that's the meaning in *square meal*. No record from any sailing vessel supports the wooden-plate theory, while print citations for *square meal* with the meaning "a good and satisfying spread" abound.

One of the most bogus of acronymic etymologies is the recurrent wheeze that *posh,* "elegant, swanky," is an acronym for "p(ort) o(ut), s(tarboard) h(ome)," a beguiling bit of linguistic legerdemain that has taken in a company of estimable scholars. When British colonial emissaries and wealthy vacationers made passage to and from India and the Orient, they often traveled along the coast of Africa on the Peninsular and Oriental Steam Navigation Company line. Many of these travelers sought ideal accommodations "away from the weather," on the more comfortable or shady side of the ship. By paying for two staterooms—one portside out, the other starboard home—the very rich could avoid the blazing sun and strong winds both ways, an act of conspicuous consumption that has become synonymous with anything luxurious and ultrasmart.

While the abundant inventiveness here deserves at least a sitting ovation, this etymology of *posh* is, well, bosh. For one thing, neither the travelers' literature of the period nor the records of the Peninsular and Oriental Steam Navigation Company show a jot of reference to *posh*. For another thing, *posh* does not show up in print until 1918.

The editors of the *Oxford English Dictionary* say nothing of any connection with the location of cabins on ships and either ignore or reject outright the acronymic theory, and the Merriam-Webster dictionaries list the origin as "unknown." More likely and more mundanely, *posh* hails from a British slang word of the same spelling that means "a dandy."

Other exhibits of CANOE, such as *between the devil and the deep blue sea* and *under the weather,* simply don't hold water and are up the creek without a paddle. In these instances non-nautical meanings are attested to long before these phrases appeared in any nautical sense, and ship's logs are devoid of the bogus seafaring definitions. Caring and careful linguists try to avoid foisting such "internetymology" on their readers, which is why I did not infect the previous chapter with such linguistic blarney.

UNDER THE WEATHER

You probably think about the weather almost every day, but have you ever noticed how much our speech is affected by weather words? Some people strike us as chilly, cool, cold, icy, or frigid, while others seem to radiate a warm and sunny disposition. Because temperature, moisture, and wind conditions are so important in our lives, a variety of weather patterns blow hot and cold through many of the descriptive phrases in our speech and writing.

The word *hurricane* blows in from the Arawakan (West Indies) name for the Caribbean god Juracán, "evil spirit of the sea." In 1953 the National Weather Service began conferring female first names on all hurricanes, categorizing those devastating winds as female. When I was a boy, we bandied about a little riddle: "Why do they give hurricanes female names?" "Because otherwise, they'd be himicanes!" Har har! Chuckle, chuckle! Snort!

That riddle doesn't make sense any longer because, in 1979, the Service started identifying hurricanes by both male and female names alternately: Alma, Bertram, Charlotte, Donald, Elaine, and so on. That's one small step for humankind. It's the right thing that those meteorological "evil spirits" not be exclusively female.

Tsunami blows in from the Japanese *tsu,* "harbor," and *nami,* "wave." Travel from the back of the word to the front, and you'll find the anagram "I am nuts!"

I truly hope that you're *on cloud nine,* meaning "in a state of high euphoria." This is a reference to the ten types of clouds defined in *International Cloud Atlas,* first published in 1896 and still in use. Cloud nine is a cumulonimbus cloud that can rise to the lofty height of 6.2 miles, as high as a cloud can be.

I also hope you won't feel that I'm *stealing your thunder.* In 1709, the English poet and playwright John Dennis quilled the tragedy *Appius and Virginia,* which turned out to be a tragic failure among critics and playgoers alike. The play bombed even though Dennis had invented for it a device that generated the roaring of thunder as part of the staging. Sadly the play generated more thunder claps than hand claps.

Shortly after the premature closing of Dennis's play, William Shakespeare's *Macbeth* came to London. Dennis attended an early performance, where he heard his own thunder machine roar during the three witches' opening scene on the heath. The upstaged Dennis exclaimed, "By God! The villains will not play my play, but they will steal my thunder!" And that's where we get the expression *steal my thunder,* meaning "to be robbed of deserved glory."

Now that you're getting acclimated to the concept of weather metaphors, complete each phrase with a word from the following weather words:

bolt	cloud	fog
breeze	cool	frozen
climate	flood	gale

hail	rain	sunny
hazy	shower	tempest
ice	slush	thunder
lightning	snow	whirlwind
misty	storm	wind

1. _____s of laughter 2. _____ in a teapot 3. _____struck
4. greased _____ 5. _____ side up

6. a _____ from the blue

7. a _____ fund 8. a _____ job 9. a _____ tour
10. a _____ of emotions 11. _____ assets 12. shoot the _____

13. brain_____ 14. break the _____ 15. get _____ of
16. take a _____ check 17. my memory of the evening
is _____ 18. I'm in a _____

19. on _____ nine 20. a _____ of bullets 21. _____ with
praise 22. a _____ cat 23. _____-eyed 24. the _____ of
opinion

Answers

1. gale 2. tempest 3. thunder 4. lightning 5. sunny 6. bolt
7. slush 8. snow 9. whirlwind 10. flood 11. frozen 12. breeze
13. storm 14. ice 15. wind 16. rain 17. hazy 18. fog
19. cloud 20. hail 21. shower 22. cool 23. misty 24. climate

Plane Talk

Two wrongs don't make a right, but two Wrights did make an airplane, and that invention has inspired the English language to fly up, up and away. Don't go into a tailspin. Straighten up and fly right by the seat of the pants ("to fly by instinct rather than instruments") on a wing and a prayer, even if you take a lot of flak. *Flak*, which seems to echo the sound of anti-aircraft shells, is adopted from the German acronym *FLeigerAbwehrKanone*, literally "pilot defense cannon."

The popular phrase "pushing the envelope" does not mean "working at a post office." The expression came into general use following the publication of Tom Wolfe's mega-selling book about the space program, *The Right Stuff:* "One of the phrases that kept running through the conversation was 'pushing the outside of the envelope' ... [That] seemed to be the great challenge and satisfaction of flight testing." Wolfe didn't originate the term, although it's appropriate that he used it in a technical and engineering context, as it was first used in the field of mathematics.

The envelope here is the mathematical envelope, the locus of the ultimate intersections of consecutive curves. That envelope describes the upper and lower limits of the various factors that it is safe to fly at, such as speed, engine power, maneuverability, wind velocity and altitude. By pushing the envelope, that is, challenging those limits, test pilots are able to determine just how far it was safe to go. The expression has now expanded beyond aeronautics to mean "to seek innovation, to stretch established limits."

As Mohith Agadi has written, "There's only one job in this world that gives you an office in the sky; and that is pilot." Before modern instruments, a pilot flew a plane based on how it felt. For example, in fog or clouds, in the absence of instrumentation a pilot could tell whether the plane was climbing or diving by how heavy he felt in the seat. Seat of the pants, first documented in 1929, is the area where one sits, i.e. the buttocks. Hence, airmen and airwomen often *flew by the seat of their pants, on a wing and a prayer.*

An ancient Roman copper coin was called an *as*, which simply meant "one," or "a unit." This meaning of "one" ultimately evolved into *ace* as the highest card in a playing deck and, in tennis, winning a point with a single serve. This embedded meaning of "topnotch" explains why an expert pilot is called an *ace.*

Helicopters don't fly; they beat the air into submission. As humorist Dave Barry, my fellow Haverford College alumnus, has written, "The truth is that helicopters are nothing at all like cars. Scientists still have no idea what holds helicopters up. Whatever it is, it could stop at any moment."

These mishmashes of whirling parts that rise up, up, and away often lighten their load by shedding their first four letters to become *copters* or their last six letters to become *helos.* Then they take flight in a sky of metaphor—*chopper, eggbeater, whirlybird, windmill, dragonfly, air bear,* and *stick buddy.* A recent metaphoric extension is the compound *helicopter parents,* which describes moms and dads who constantly hover above their children's lives and activities.

Please note that *fly by night,* as in "a fly-by-night business," is not an aviation expression. Here *fly* simply means "run away, flee" under cover of darkness. On the other wing, *fly by wire* is a fairly new term in aviation. Nowadays, the cockpit (named from the cramped arena of flying feathers where cockfights take place) controls on large aircraft aren't balled throttles but electronic devices that talk to electric motors in the wings and tail via digital circuitry. Hence, *fly by wire*

Balls to the wall (no lawsuits, please!) is an aviation metaphor that means "an all-out effort." On airplanes, the handles controlling the throttle and the fuel mixture are often topped with ball-shaped grips. Pushing those grips forward, close to the front wall of the cockpit, increases the amount of fuel going to the engines and generates the highest possible speed. As some airborne jester wrote, "If you push the stick forward, the houses get bigger. If you pull the stick back, they get smaller. Unless you keep pulling the stick back. Then they get bigger again."

Racing with the Moon, Dancing with the Stars

So far in this thematic cluster, the sky's been the limit. Now let's soar up, up, and away to outer space.

I'm over the moon about moon words. Have you ever wondered why the words *lunatic* and *lunar* begin with the same four letters? Etymology supplies the answer. *Lunatic* derives from *luna,* Latin for "moon," which when it is full, is said to render us daft—*moonstruck* and *loony.*

We keep time with the moon. *Monday* began as Old English for "moon day," and *month,* again from Old English, is the duration between full moons, the time it takes our lunar satellite to complete its voyage around our planet.

A *honeymoon* is an early harmony in any relationship, especially marriage. Here we come to the juncture of "honey" and the long-ago way of saying "month": *moon.* The first month of marriage is often the sweetest, but just when the moon is full and bright, it begins to wane as can sadly happen with matrimony.

The opportunity to read an explanation about the phrase *once in a blue moon* comes along once in a blue moon, when pigs fly, and hell freezes over and scarce as hens' teeth and lips on a chicken. Among these metaphors for very rare occurrences, *blue moon* is the most colorful.

A blue moon is the second full moon in a single month, a phenomenon that occurs, well, once in a blue moon. These bonus full moons present themselves on average once every 2.7 years. The expression has nothing to do with the actual color of the moon, but whenever certain natural conditions align, such as volcanic eruptions or titanic fires sending particles into the atmosphere, the moon can actually appear to be tinged with blue.

Some of us distill or drink *moonshine* ("illegal liquor") or babble *moonshine* ("nonsense"). Some of us *moonlight* with a second job that we perform at night. Others of us *moon* over a desired lover. Then there's that other verb *to moon*. I'll leave you to figure out how that act got its name.

Moving right along to another body part, that whitish crescent at the base of each of your fingernails (none on your toenails) actually has a name—*lunule* or *lunula,* French-Latin for "little moon."

Scientists got tired of watching the moon go around the earth for twenty-four hours. They decided to call it a day.

Have you ever dined at the restaurant on the moon? The food is great, but the place doesn't have any atmosphere.

After those moonstruck, loony jokes, let's go dancing with the stars, which eclipse the moon when it comes to the intensity of the light they shine upon English words. In an astronomical number of ways, the English language sees stars. We are so starstruck and starry-eyed that we call our stage, screen, and athletic celebrities stars. May this verbivorous book be a *lodestar* ("way" + "star"), a source of inspiration in your life. A lodestar is used in navigation to show the way.

A Latin word for "star" is *stella,* whence the adjective *stellar,* the noun *constellation,* and name *Stella.* Another starry Latin word part is *astrum*, a prolific root that gives us *aster* ("a flower with star-shaped petals"), *astrology* ("star study"), *astronomer* ("star arranger"), *asteroid* ("star form"), and *astronaut* ("star sailor"). An asterisk is a symbol that looks like a "little star." You may wish to dispute these celestial etymologies, but I think you'd be an asterisk it.

In William Shakespeare's *Julius Caesar*, Cassius warns that "the fault, dear Brutus, lies not in our stars, but in ourselves." Nevertheless, for centuries, people have believed that the stars and their heavenly positions govern events on earth. If the conjunction of the stars is not propitious, disaster will strike. Created from the Latin *dis* ("bad, against") and *astrum*, *disaster* literally means "against the stars"—ill-starred, star-crossed. In the ghostly opening scene of *Hamlet*, Horatio speaks of "stars with trains of fire and dews of blood, disasters in the sun."

Astrologers used to study the stars to see how their coming together at a person's birth would influence his or her future. *Desire* is star-spun from the Latin *de*, "from," + *sidus*, "star." The idea is that we wish for and desire fortunate outcomes that stream from our lucky stars. In the same constellation is *consider*, which radiates from the Latin *cum*, "with" + *sidera*, "stars." The first meaning of *consider* was "to examine stars together to gauge their effects on our fate."

The influence of the stars reposes even within the word *influence* itself. *Influence* originally meant a flowing or streaming from the stars of an ethereal fluid that acted upon the character and destiny of human beings.

The ancients also believed that the influence of a star generated the *dog days*, summer periods of triple *h* weather—hazy, hot, and humid. In the days of the Romans, the six or eight hottest weeks of the summer, roughly July through the first half of August, were known colloquially as *caniculares dies*, or "days of the dog." According to Roman lore, the dog star Sirius rose with and added its heat to the sun, making a hot time of the year even hotter.

Galaxy, a Greek through Latin word that describes ginormous, humongous clusters of stars, originally meant "milky," as in *lactose* and *lactic*. We call our galaxy the Milky Way.

Derived from Greek *ekkentros*, "out of the center," from *ek*, "out of" + *kentron*, "center," *eccentric* first appeared in English in 1551 as an astronomical term describing "a circle in which a heavenly body deviates from its center." Modern-day astronomers still use *eccentric* in that way.

Greek also bequeaths us *zodiakos*, "circle of little animals." *Zodiac* is the ancient Greek name for the heavenly belt of twelve signs believed to influence human behavior. The *zo-* in *zodiac* is related to the *zo-* in *zoo* and *zoology*—"life."

Truth be told, I'm a Gemini, so I don't believe in astrology.

☺When Metaphors Collide

In the opening cluster of this book you saw how we figuratively compare an emotionally lacerating experience to how a farm harrow pulverizes the earth, how we liken the shape of a tulip to a turban, how we coalesce starting up a conversation with breaking ice, and how we equate the whitish crescent at the base of each of our fingernails with a little moon.

These comparisons are called metaphors. A metaphor (the word originally meant "carry beyond" in Greek) is a figure of speech that merges two objects or ideas that are, for the most part, different from each other but turn out to be alike in some significant way. In other words, metaphors tell it like it isn't to show us what it really is.

Metaphors are the cat's pajamas and the cat's meow. They help us break the ice, bury the hatchet, blow off steam, and raise the bar for what makes colorful language. Without metaphors, we're a day late and a dollar short, out in left field, up the creek without a paddle, skating on thin ice, and falling into hot water.

Unfortunately, the strength of the metaphor is also its weakness. Because they're used so often and because so many of them sound or seem so much alike, it's easy to accidentally jumble two of them together, even when you *aren't* a bubble off plumb and three sheets to the wind. Flying in the face of physics, two metaphors *can* occupy the same space at the same time.

Should you ever realize that you've promiscuously mixed your metaphors, don't feel as if you laid an egg, have egg on your face or that you're walking on eggshells, or are sucking eggs. After all, sometimes that's just the way the cookie falls where it may, as we see when metaphors collide. Every mixed-up metaphor that follows is genuine, certified, and authentic. I swear on a stack of dictionaries that I have not concocted any of them. I hope that they will kindle in you a flood of laughter:

- She has a mind like a steel sieve.
- That's a horse of a different color.
- The sacred cows have come home to roost.
- The communist menace is a snake in the grass that is gnawing away at the foundation of our ship of state.
- She was a diva of such immense talent that, after she performed, there was seldom a dry seat in the house.
- He came through the experience smelling like a knight in shining armor.
- We are in a butt-ugly recession right now, but we are seeing light at the end of the tunnel.
- The bankers' pockets are bulging with the sweat of the honest working man.
- They're biting the hand of the goose that laid the golden egg.
- A virgin forest is a place where the hand of man has never set foot.
- My crew cut made my ears stick out like a sore thumb.
- She kept breaking through the glass ceiling and that ruffled some feathers. "There were too many people looking to throw darts," she said.
- The president hit the bull's eye on the nose.

- The media report violent events, which leads others to become violent. That leads to more reporting, which brings on still more violence. It's a vicious snowball.
- My mother literally worked like a Trojan horse to put me through college.
- They pulled the plug out from under me.
- Fish or get off the pot.
- Don't worry. I've got an ace up my hole.
- Let's jump off that bridge when we come to it.
- Don't count all your chickens in one basket.
- Now the shoe is on the horse of a different color.
- She's robbing Peter to pay the piper.
- He's up a tree without a paddle.
- Keep your ear to the grindstone.
- Sometimes you've gotta stick your neck out on a limb.

That's the whole kettle of fish in a nutshell. So let's grab the bull by the tail and look it directly in the eye. This isn't rocket surgery. When you boil it right down to brass tacks, it's best to avoid mixing up your metaphors.

THAT'S ENTERTAINMENT!

FACE THE MUSIC

William Shakespeare began his comedy *Twelfth Night* with the line "If music be the food of love, play on!" About a century later, the playwright William Congreve opened his comedy *The Mourning Bride* with the equally famous line "Music has charms to soothe a savage breast" (almost always misquoted as "the savage beast").

If music be the food of love, it is also the food of language. Music has charms that teem our tongues, course through our pens, and luminesce up on our computer screens.

I am often asked to be a keynote speaker. I don't speak to trumpet my accomplishments, blow my own horn, or drum up business for my books. Rather, I come to set the proper key and the proper note and to strike a responsive chord. A keynote speaker delivers a keynote address in which he or she develops the underlying theme of a gathering. The term *keynote* began with the practice of playing a note before a group, such as a barbershop quartet, started singing a cappella. The note sounded determined the key in which the song would be performed; thus the term *keynote*.

Keynote is one word in a symphony of musical metaphors that sing throughout our everyday vocabulary. Aria ready to face the music? Of chorus you are. Many actors experience a touch of stage fright at the moment of going onstage.

But, looking out across the orchestra pit, each performer must *face the music,* as I now ask you to do.

You may feel that there's too much sax and violins in my writing. You may think me a Johnny-one-note who doesn't know my brass from my oboe. But all I can say to that is "Fiddlesticks! I've got an upbeat attitude. I'm feeling fit as a fiddle, and I don't fiddle around or play second fiddle to anybody."

I'm a one-man band, and I march to the beat of a different drummer. I'm not going to give you a second-string performance or play it by ear or harp on the subject. Rather, I'm an unsung hero who's going to pull out all the stops and not soft-pedal any aspect of our melodious, mellifluous English language.

Second-string originally meant a set of violin strings kept on hand in case the strings in the instrument broke. When we talk or write about someone *soft-pedaling* something, we are referring to the soft pedal on a piano that is used to modify the timbre. When we soft-pedal an idea, we moderate and play it down. If, on the other hand, we do the opposite and *pull out all the stops*, we are like an organist who pulls out all the knobs (stops) in the organ to bring all the pipes into play.

To harp on, meaning "to dwell on the same topic," is a shortening of the old phrase *to harp on one string,* which meant "to play one note on a harp string over and over." A student once wrote, "In the Bible, David was a Hebrew king skilled at playing the liar." The budding scholar meant *lyre.* The lyre was a harp-like instrument played by the ancient Greeks. *Lyre* bequeaths us the words *lyric* and *lyrical.*

I, your unsung hero, will now waltz out of here without missing a beat—not on a sour note but on a high note. Please remember that I'm not just whistling Dixie, and I don't mean to chime in and harp on this subject to beat the band. Sure, I'm all keyed up and jazzed up, but I'm not here to give you a song and dance or create a cheap soap opera that draws a chorus of boos. In this book, nobody has to pay the piper.

Rather, I'm trying to steal the show and orchestrate an overture so that we can ring in a harmonious relationship, get in tune with each other, and hop on the same bandwagon. Then you'll sing a different tune, and we can make beautiful music together.

Show Biz in the Limelight

Because entertainment is such a joyful, enriching part of our world, show business metaphors help our language to *get its act together* and *get the show on the road.* At the opportune moment, these sprightly words and expressions stop *waiting in the wings* and *step out into the limelight.* The first limelights were theatrical spotlights that used heated calcium oxide, or quicklime, to give off a light that was brilliant and white but not hot. Ever since that bright idea, *to be in the limelight* has been a metaphor for being in the glare of public scrutiny. Such show biz metaphors become *a tough act to follow.*

Break a leg is a cliché well-wishers say ironically to actors, singers, and musicians before they go on stage to perform. The origin of the imperative is obscure. One theory shifts the meaning of the word *break*, claiming that the expression means "May you take so many bows that the line of your leg will break multiply at the knee as the audience continues to applaud." This interpretation is supported by the expression *make a leg*, "to make a deep bow with the right leg drawn back," which started in the late sixteenth century.

Slapstick comedy owes its name to the double lath that clowns in seventeenth-century pantomimes wielded. The terrific sound of the two flat wooden sticks slapping together on the harlequin's derriere banged out the word *slapstick.*

One of the puppet clowns who did the slapping was Punch, forever linked to his straightwoman Judy. The Punch that is so pleased in the cliché *pleased as Punch* is not the sweet stuff we quaff. That phrase, in fact, alludes to the cheerful singing and self-satisfaction of the manic puppet Punch.

From the art of puppetry we gain another expression. Puppet masters manipulate the strings of their marionettes from behind a dark curtain. Unseen, they completely control the actions of their on-stage actors. Whence the expression *to pull strings.*

For my closing act, I shine the spotlight on a few show-stopping words that were born backstage and onstage:

Claptrap was originally a theatrical trick designed to attract (*trap*) applause (*clap*) in a theater. It might have been a showy line, such as "Britannia rules the waves!" Thus, *claptrap* compares a clap trapper to a shallow, showy, cheap sentiment expressed solely for effect.

Playwrights, novelists, screenwriters, and other storytellers involve their characters in a plot in which they become tied in a knot woven from the complicated threads of the storyline. The *denouement,* from the French *desnouer,* "to untie," is the outcome of the plot complications that have bound the characters.

Desultory jumps down from the Latin *de-,* "from," and *salire,* "to leap." The Roman *desultors,* or leapers, were circus performers who performed the feat of jumping from one galloping horse to another. They were soon compared with people who fitfully jumped from one idea to another in conversation or one goal to another in their lives.

Explode comes from the Latin *explodere,* "to chase away by clapping one's hands." In ancient Rome, audiences were terrifically active in expressing their praise or disapproval of actors. Disgruntled theatergoers would clap loudly to show their dissatisfaction with the performance on stage. (To show approval, ancient Romans would wave the flap of their togas.)

Hanky-panky is possibly created, with the aid of reduplication, from the magician's handkerchief, or "hanky," a prop for trickery and sleight of hand. Or *hanky-panky* may be an alteration of *hocus-pocus.*

Hypocrite is an offspring of the Greek *hypokrites,* a stage actor who, by the nature of his occupation, often wore a mask and pretended to be someone other than himself. By extension, a hypocrite pretends to beliefs or feelings he doesn't really have. *Person* also steps from the stage into our everyday parlance. In Greek and Roman theater, actors played more than one role during a performance simply by donning a *persona* ("mask") to change character. Eventually, *persona* came to mean the role an individual assumes in life and, later, the individual himself.

The ancient Athenian playwright, producer, and stage director Thespis is often dubbed the Father of Greek Tragedy. Until his time, dramatic presentations in Greece consisted entirely of singing by a chorus. Thespis is said to have innovated, in 534 B.C., the connection of the chorus directly to the plot and the role of the very first actor by having a member of the chorus step forward and carry on a dialogue with the other members. We remember his name in the word *thespian,* "actor."

You're a real trouper to have stayed with this lesson in etymology to the final curtain call. Note that the spelling isn't the military *trouper,* but *trouper,* a member of a theater company. *A real trouper* now means "one who perseveres through hardship without complaint."

A Circus of Words

When you say or write *a three-ring circus*, you are actually repeating yourself because *circus* echoes *kirkos*, the Greek word for "ring, circle."In 2017, after 146 years of bedazzling Americans from California to the New York island, the Ringling Bros. and Barnum & Bailey Circus folded its tents. Pulled by dwindling attendance and mounting operating costs, the final curtain came down on the Greatest Show on Earth:

> Nothing now to mark the spot
>   But a littered vacant lot.
> Sawdust in a heap, and where
>   The center ring stood, grass worn bare.
>
> But remain the sounds and sights—
>   The artists, music, beasts, and lights.
> May the spangled memories soar
>   In our hearts forevermore.

But a number of smaller circuses endure, and their special vocabulary stays alive. Communities are most likely to develop a colorful argot when they have limited contact with the world outside of their group. The circus community is a perfect example of the almost monastic self-containment in which argot flourishes. Big top people travel in very close quarters, and because they usually go into a town, set up, do a show, tear down, and leave, they have little contact with the locals. They socialize with each other, they intermarry, and their children acquire the argot from the time they start to talk.

"Hey, First-of-May! Tell the butcher in the back yard to stay away from the bulls, humps, stripes, and painted ponies. We have some cherry pie for him before doors and spec." Sound like doubletalk? Actually, that's circus talk—or, more technically, circus argot, argot being a specialized vocabulary used by a particular group for mutual bonding and private communication.

First-of-May designates anyone who is brand-new to circus work. That's because circuses used to start their tours around the first day in May. A *candy butcher* is a concessionaire who sells cotton candy (*floss*) and other food, along with drinks and souvenirs, to the audience during the show. The *backyard* is the place just behind the circus entrance where performers wait to do their acts. A *bull* is a circus elephant, even though most of them are female. Among other circus beasts, *humps, stripes,* and *painted ponies* are, respectively, camels, tigers, and zebras. *Cherry pie* is extra work, probably from *chairy pie,* the setting up of extra chairs around the arena. *Doors!* is the cry that tells circus folk that the audience is coming in to take their seats, and *spec* is short for *spectacle,* the big parade of all the performers.

Trust me: This topic ain't no *dog and pony show*—the designation for a small circus with just a few acts, also known as a *mud show.*

What we call the toilet circus folk call the *donniker,* the hot dog or grill concession trailer where the circus people can snag a snack is a *grease joint,* and a circus performer is a *kinker.* The townspeople are *towners* or *rubes.* In the old days, when large groups of towners who believed (sometimes accurately) that they had been fleeced by dishonest circus people, they would come back in a mob to seek retribution. The cry *Hey rube!* went out, and everyone knew that the fight was on.

When a circus came to town, the sheriff would often remove the nut from a wheel of the main wagon. Because in bygone days these nuts were elaborately and individually crafted, they were well-nigh impossible to replace. Thus, the circus couldn't leave town until the costs of land, utilities, rental, easements, and security were paid. It's but a short metaphorical leap to the modern meaning of *making the nut,* "meeting one's expenses."

Close, but no cigar is a twentieth-century American phrase that alludes to the workers in circus and carnival booths who awarded cigars as prizes. The expression applied to those who were close to winning a prize, but failed to do so; that is, "just short of being perfect."

A full house is called a *straw house* from the days when straw would be laid down in front of the seats to accommodate more people than the seats could hold. Distances between engagements were called *jumps.* Thus, an old circus toast rings out: "May your lots be grassy, your jumps short, and your houses straw."

Ladies and gentlemen! Children of all ages! For my closing act, I present two stories:

At the end of the nineteenth century, a crisis arose in the Barnum and Bailey Circus. The man who was shot out of the cannon every day was asked by his wife to quit his high-risk profession, much to the distress of Phineas Taylor Barnum, "the Greatest Showman on Earth." P.T., whose wit was equal to his showmanship, summoned the fellow and said, "I beg you to reconsider. Men of your caliber are hard to find." Barnum, of course, was perpetrating a playful pun on the word *caliber*, which, from its earliest beginnings, meant "the diameter of a bullet or other projectile."

Egress, from the Latin *e*, "out" + *gress*, "step," is a fancy word for exit, and P. T. Barnum, made creative use of it.

Barnum's American Museum in Lower Manhattan was so popular that it attracted up to fifteen thousand customers daily, and some would spend the entire day there. This cut into profits, as the museum would be too full to squeeze another person in. In classic Barnum style, P. T. put up above a cage holding a mother tiger and her cubs a sign that read, TIGRESS Then, over a doorway next to that sign, he put up another sign that said, TO THE EGRESS. Many customers followed that sign, looking for an exhibit featuring an exotic female bird. What they found instead was themselves out the door ("the Egress") and back on the street. Once they had exited the building, the door would lock behind them, and if they wanted to get back in, they had to pay another admission charge.

☺ THE PALINDROMEDARY

A palindrome, from two Greek roots that mean "to run forward and backward," is a word or statement that reads the same forward and backward. Even if you're a dud, kook, boob, or poop, palindromes should make you exult, "Ah ha!, Oh, ho!, Hey, yeh!, Yo boy!, Yay!, Wow!"

Here's an exclusive interview I conducted with the Palindromedary himself, the two-way statement made flesh. This camel is a talking animal smitten with Ailihphilia—the love of palindromes. Everything the Palindromedary says is a WORD ROW. YA, WOW! TWO-WAY WORD ROW that reads both ways.

LEDERER: So you're the famous Palindromedary.

PALINDROMEDARY: I, MALE, MACHO, OH, CAMEL AM I.

I see that, despite your fame, you're wearing a name tag. Why?

GATEMAN SEES NAME. GARAGEMAN SEES NAME TAG.

Is it true that you were discovered in the Nile region?

CAMEL IN NILE, MAC.

I heard that the trainer said an earful to the flying elephant in your menagerie. What was the trainer's command?

    "DUMBO, LOB MUD."

I hear Dan, the lion tamer, is sick in bed.

    POOR DAN IS IN A DROOP.

Is anybody treating Dan?

    DR. AWKWARD.

So there won't be a lion performance today?

    NO, SIT! CAT ACT IS ON.

What was the last act you saw?

    OH WHO WAS IT I SAW, OH WHO?

Well, have you seen the big cats in action?

    WAS IT A CAR OR A CAT I SAW?

Why won't we be witnessing the performing dog?

    A DOG? A PANIC IN A PAGODA!

Where do you keep the dogs?

    POOCH COOP.

I heard that somebody slipped something into the dog cage.

    GOD! A RED NUGGET! A FAT EGG UNDER A DOG!

The menagerie includes gnus. Did those gnus actually sing the *Star Spangled Banner?*
> RISE, NUT! GNUS SUNG TUNE, SIR.

What about the rumor that one of the gnus is ill?
> UNGASTROPERITONITIS—IS IT I? NOT I, REPORTS A GNU.

What's the problem when you come after the gnu act?
> GNU DUNG.

What happened when you followed the dog act?
> DID I STEP ON DOG DOO? GOOD GOD! NO PETS! I DID!

Why aren't the owls performing tonight?
> TOO HOT TO HOOT.

And the panda?
> PANDA HAD NAP.

And the elk?
> ELK CACKLE.

And the rat?
> OOZY RAT IN A SANITARY ZOO.

And the deer?
> DEER FRISK, SIR, FREED.

Did you see Kay and her yak?
> KAY, A RED NUDE, PEEPED UNDER A YAK.

Is it also true that you sewed a dress for the kangaroo?
I MADE KANGAROO TUTU. TOO RAG-NAKED AM I.

What's one of your favorite human circus acts?
TRAPEZE PART.

And what's especially exciting about the trapeze?
TEN ON TRAPEZE PART! NO NET!

No net?
NO TENT NET ON.

You seem truly excited about the circus.
AVID AS A DIVA.

Are there any acts that you would get rid of?
DUDE, NOT ONE DUD.

But what do you say to those who contend that the circus can't survive as an art form?
"NO! IT CAN! ACTION!"

Mr. Palindromedary, we thank you for such a scintillating two-way interview. Is it true that you are the only animal who can speak intelligibly in palindromes?
YES, THAT'S TRUE. ALL OTHER ANIMALS SAY THINGS LIKE *"EKILS GNIH TYASS LAMINAR EHTOLLAE URTSTAHT SEY."*

My Kids, the Poker Players

As luck would have it, you're reading a book written by one of the most successful breeders of world-class poker professionals ever. My son, Howard "The Professor" Lederer, and daughter, Annie "The Duchess of Poker" Duke, have taken home eleven and a half million dollars in poker championships. They are the first sibling pair to have reached the final table of a World Series of Poker event, and both have won WSOP bracelets.

My children's achievements in the gaming halls inspire me to deal from a full deck of vivid words and phrases that have made the journey from the poker table into our everyday conversation and writing. The colorful and high-risk excitement of poker have made the language of the game among the most pervasive metaphors in our everyday parlance.

The basic elements of poker are the cards, the chips, and the play of the hand. Each has become embedded in our daily parlance. Beginning with the cards, the verb *to discard* descends from *decard*, "away card," and first meant to throw away a card from one's hand. Gradually, the meaning of *discard* broadened to include rejection beyond card playing. A cardsharp who is out to cheat you may be dealing from the bottom of the deck and giving you a fast shuffle, in which case you may get lost in the shuffle.

You might call a low-down skunk *a four-flusher. Flush,* a hand of five cards of a single suit, flows from the Latin *fluxus,* "flow." A *four-flusher* characterizes a poker player who pretends to such good fortune but in fact holds a worthless hand of only four same-suit cards. If you don't know that a flush beats a straight, you will be flush-straighted at a poker table.

The cleverest application of poker terminology that I've encountered appears on the sides of some plumbing trucks: "A Flush Is Better Than a Full House." In poker that isn't true, but a homeowner would recognize its wisdom.

Now that I've laid my cards on the table, let's see what happens when the chips are down. Why do we call a gilt-edged, sure-thing stock *a blue-chip stock?* Because the blue chips have traditionally been the most valuable. Why, when we compare the value of two things, do we often ask how one *stacks up* against the other, as in "How do the Cardinals stack up against the Yankees?" Here the reference is to the columns of chips piled up before the players around a poker table. These stacks also account for the compound *bottom dollar. Betting one's bottom dollar* means wagering your entire stack right down to the felt. The metaphor of poker chips is so powerful that one of the euphemisms we use for death is *cashing in your chips.*

The guts of poker is the betting. *I'm all in,* risking your entire chip stack in one bet, has recently become a standard affirmative in American English, traveling from the game of No-Limit Texas Hold'em to our everyday vocabulary. If your opponents wish to call your bluff and insist that you put up or shut up, you'll be happy to put your money where your mouth is. Rather than passing the buck, maintain an inscrutable poker face, play it close to the vest, and hope to hit the jackpot.

Jackpot originally described the reward to the big winner in a game of progressive poker. In this game, you need a pair of jacks or better to "open the pot," and the stakes grow higher until the requisite pair is dealt. *Jackpot* has gradually expanded to include the pots of gold in slot machines, game shows, and state lotteries.

Pass the buck is a cliché that means "to shift responsibility," but why should handing someone a dollar indicate that a duty is transferred? Once again, the answer can be found in long-ago gambling pleasure palaces. The *buck* in *pass the buck* was originally a hunting knife whose handle was made from a buck's horn. The knife was placed in front of the player to the left of the dealer who had to bet first, a position of liability. That knife gave the game its name—Buckhorn Poker or Buck Poker—and gave us the expression *pass the buck*. After each deal, the buck was passed from the first wagerer to the next player, changing the buck-passer's position from one of disadvantage to one of advantage.

In the Old West, silver dollars often replaced buckhorn knives as tokens, and these coins took on the slang name *buck*. President Harry S. Truman, reputed to be a skillful poker player, adopted the now-famous motto "The buck stops here," meaning that the ultimate responsibility rests with the president.

You can bet on it.

WE ALL SPEAK MOVIE LINES

Americans have fallen deeply in love with that beguiling conspiracy of light and darkness and color and silence and sound and music that we call the movies. In the movie theater and on smaller screens the boundaries between real and reel, the line between reality and movies, wavers and blurs. Something has happened to our American language—and we've a feeling we're not in Kansas anymore.

You probably recognize the second part of that statement as a borrowing from the iconic film *The Wizard of Oz*. Being transported out of Kansas is one of a passel of expressions from movies that have launched a thousand lips.

The first Academy Awards ceremony took place during a banquet held in the Blossom Room of the Hollywood Roosevelt Hotel. When the first awards were handed out on May 16, 1929, movies had just begun to talk. Two hundred and seventy attended, tickets cost ten dollars, and the awards part of the evening lasted fifteen minutes. I would love to have been a time traveler rushing into the Blossom Room to announce the luminous future of the movie industry.

So let's cut to the chase, an expression that refers to chase scenes in action movies. The literal use, as a director's instruction to transition to a chase scene, is almost a century old. A 1929 screenplay, for example, includes "Jannings escapes. Cut to chase." Ultimately, the idiom evolved from "enough of the kissy-kissy scene already; let's get to the car chase" to a more figurative use: "Get to the point." That extended meaning is fairly recent, dating from only the early 1980s.

"Wait a minute! Wait a minute! You ain't heard nothin' yet!" That's what Al Jolson said in *The Jazz Singer* (1927), the mother of all talking films. Ever since, lines from the movies have shaped our hopes and dreams and aspirations and have suffused our everyday conversations.

Today I'm making you an offer you can't refuse—a version of the line in Mario Puzo's novel, *The Godfather* (1969) and the ensuing1972 film.

So, "what's up, Doc?" That, of course, is Bugs Bunny's question to Elmer Fudd. What's up is that I hope never to hear from my readers, "What we got here is a failure to communicate" or "I'm mad as hell, and I'm not going to take this anymore!" The first statement began as Strother Martin's line in *Cool Hand Luke*, and the second is Peter Finch's furious protest in *Network*.

May you never sneer at me, "Frankly, my dear. I don't give a damn," spoken by Clark Gable in *Gone with the Wind*. Just remember that "tomorrow is another day," spoken by Vivien Leigh in the same film.

"I think this is the beginning of a beautiful friendship" is a line delivered by Humphrey Bogart in *Casablanca*. That film also bequeaths us "Round up the usual suspects," "Here's looking at you, kid," and the oft misquoted "Play it, Sam."

Read on, and "make my day"—the signature statement of the Clint Eastwood character Dirty Harry in the 1983 film *Sudden Impact*.

"Who you gonna call?"—your faithful language author! That's a snippet from *Ghostbusters,* and, of course, it should be "*whom* are you going to call?"

52

WE ALL SPEAK MOVIE LINES

Now let's cut to the chase with a groovy movie game. Now identify the movies whence come the following filmic expressions that inhabit our everyday conversations:

1. They're ba-a-a-ck! 2. If you build it, they will come. 3. Houston, we have a problem. 4. Greed is good. 5. You talkin' to me?

6. I coulda been a contender. 7. Why don't you come up and see me sometime? 8. Rosebud. 9. May the Force be with you! 10. Show me the money!

11. Love means never having to say you're sorry. 12. Heeeeere's Johnny! 13. There's no crying in baseball! 14. I'm the king of the world! 15. You're gonna need a bigger boat.

16. It was Beauty killed the Beast. 17. Win just one for the Gipper. 18. Who's on first. 19. They call me Mister Tibbs 20. I'll have what she's having.

21. E. T. phone home. 22. I love the smell of napalm in the morning. 23. Plastics. 24. Shaken, not stirred. 25. I want to be alone.

Answers

1. *Poltergeist* 2. *Field of Dreams* 3. *Apollo 13* 4. *Wall Street* 5. *Taxi Driver*

6. *On the Waterfront* 7. *She Done Him Wrong* 8. *Citizen Kane* 9. *Star Wars* 10. *Jerry Maguire*

11. *Love Story* 12. *The Shining* 13. *A League of Their Own* 14. *Titanic* 15. *Jaws*

16. *King Kong* 17. *Knute Rockne All-American* 18. *The Naughty Nineties* 19. *In the Heat of the Night* 20. *When Harry Met Sally*

21. *E.T. the Extra-Terrestrial* 22. *Apocalypse Now* 23. *The Graduate* 24. *Doctor No* 25. *Grand Hotel*

Finally, two lines that got their start in Merry Melodies and *Terminator 2: Judgment Day*—That's all, folks! Hasta la vista, baby!

FOOD FOR THOUGHT

WE SAY A MOUTHFUL

As a devout Foodist, I'm pleased to serve you a bountiful banquet of culinary word origins.

Both our food and our language are peppered with salt. The ancients knew that salt was essential to a good diet, and centuries before artificial refrigeration, it was the only chemical that could preserve meat. Thus, a portion of the wages paid to Roman soldiers was "salt money," with which to buy salt, derived from the Latin, *sal*. This stipend came to be called a *salarium*, from which we acquire the word *salary*. A loyal and effective soldier was quite literally worth his salt.

Salt seasons not only the word *salary,* but also the words *salad, salsa, sausage,* and *salami.* You don't have to take my etymological explanations with a grain of salt. That is, you, who are the salt of the earth, don't need to sprinkle salt on my word stories to find them palatable. They're already worth their salt.

If you know where the Big Apple is, why don't you know where the Minneapolis?—which raises the question "Whence cometh the phrase *Big Apple*, referring to New York City?"

The first print citation shows up in 1921 in a regular racing column in the *New York Morning Telegraph* by one

John Fitz Gerald, in which he used "big apple" to refer to the race tracks of New York. By 1924, Fitz Gerald had broadened the phrase to identify the city itself: "The Big Apple, the dream of every lad that ever threw a leg over a thoroughbred. There's only one Big Apple. That's New York." The columnist wrote that he had first heard the phrase from two Black stable hands in New Orleans in 1920, for whom "the big apple" was their name for the New York racetracks—the big time, "the goal of every aspiring jockey and trainer."

The cakewalk was originally a nineteenth-century entertainment invented by African Americans in the antebellum South. It was intended to satirize the stiff ballroom promenades of White plantation owners, who favored the rigidly formal dances of European high society. Cakewalking slaves lampooned these stuffy moves by accentuating their high kicks, bows, and imaginary hat doffings, mixing the cartoonish gestures together with traditional African steps. Likely unaware of the dance's derisive roots, the Whites often invited their slaves to participate in Sunday contests, to determine which dancers were most elegant and inventive. The winners would receive a piece of cake, a prize that became the dance's familiar name. Doesn't that just *take the cake*?

After Emancipation, the contest tradition continued in Black communities; the *Oxford English Dictionary* dates the widespread adoption of *cakewalk* to the late 1870s. It was around this time that the *cakewalk* came to mean "an easy task"—not because the dance was particularly simple to do but because of its languid pace and association with weekend leisure.

Close cousin to cake is pie. In days of yore, housewives often needed to scrimp, even on essentials. Whenever wheat was in short supply, the bottom crust of pies was made with rye meal. Wheat was used only for the *upper crust*. Soon *upper crust* entered everyday speech to mean "the socially select."

Eating humble pie has nothing etymologically to do with the word *humble*, "lowly." The dish was really *umble pie*, a pie stuffed with the chopped or minced part of an animal's "pluck"—the heart, lungs, liver, and other innards—especially of a deer. While the lord of the manor and the upper crust feasted on a delectable haunch of venison, the gamekeeper and other servants had to settle for edible viscera.

In the cake and pie family is bread. *Companion* derives from the Latin *com*, "together," and *panis,* "bread." You and I are companions who break the bread of language together. Breaking bread was an important ritual of welcome and hospitality. Hence, the word *company*.

That wage earners are called breadwinners reminds us of the importance of bread in medieval life. Not surprisingly, both *lord* and *lady* are well-bread words. *Lord* descends from the Old English *hlaf*, "loaf" + *weard*, "keeper," and *lady* from *hlaf*, "loaf," + *dige*, "kneader." *Pumpernickel* is etymologically baked from the German *pumpern*, "to break wind," + *Nickel*, "devil, demon, goblin." The idea is that those who eat the heavy, dark, hard-to-digest rye bread are liable to be smitten by a diabolical flatulence.

So here's a toast to all those flavorful metaphors that add spice to our English language. Does that use of *toast* relate etymologically to the familiar slice of heated bread? In a word, yes. In the days of Queen Elizabeth I and William Shakespeare, it was common practice to dip a piece of spiced toast into the bottom of one's tankard of ale or glass of sack (a bitter sherry) to improve the flavor and remove the impurities. The libation itself thus became "a toast," as did the gesture of drinking to another's health.

I close with a toast to you, my fellow wordaholic, logolept, and verbivore: "Here's champagne to our real friends, and real pain to our sham friends!" Thank you for being a real friend of our glorious, uproarious, victorious, courageous, outrageous, contagious, stupendous, tremendous, end-over-endous English language!

☺WE EAT OUR WORDS

Not long ago, Steve Jobs was alive, Johnny Cash was alive, and Bob Hope was alive. Now we have no jobs, no cash, and no hope. Let us pray that Meatloaf, Kevin Bacon, and Jon Hamm do not die.

Now it's time to nibble on a spicy, meaty, juicy topic that I know you'll savor and relish. I'm talking about a full plate, the whole enchilada—an overflowing smorgasbord.

Feast your eyes on the veritable banquet of mushrooming food expressions that grace the table of our English language and season our tongue. As we chew the fat about the food-filled phrases that are packed like sardines and sandwiched into our everyday conversations, I'll sweeten the pot with some tidbits of food for thought.

I know what's eating you. I've heard through the grapevine that you don't give a fig about me because you think I'm nutty as a fruitcake and have gone crackers and bananas; that you're fed up with me for biting off more than I can chew; that you want me to drop this subject like a hot potato because I'm a spoiled-rotten weenie in a pickle; and that you're giving me the raspberry for asking you to swallow a cheesy, corny, mushy, saccharine, seedy, soupy, sugarcoated, syrupy topic that just isn't your cup of tea.

Okay, so you're beet red with anger that I'm feeding you a bunch of baloney, garbage, and tripe; that I'm making you ruminate on a potboiler that's no more than a tempest in a teapot; that I've upset your apple cart by rehashing an old chestnut that's just pie in the sky and won't amount to a hill of beans; that you want to chew me out for buttering you up and putting words in your mouth; and that you're simmering because you think I'm an out-to-lunch bad apple who's out to egg you on.

But nuts to all that. That's the way the cookie crumbles. Eat your heart out and stop crying in your beer. I'm going to stop mincing words, start cooking with gas, take my idea off the back burner, and bring home the bacon without hamming it up. No matter how you slice it, this fruitful, tasteful topic is the icing on the cake and the greatest thing since sliced bread.

Rather than crying over spilt milk and leaping out of the frying pan into the fire, I'm going to put all my eggs in one basket, take potluck, and spill the beans. I'm cool as a cucumber and confident that this crackerjack, peachy-keen feast that I've cooked up will have you eating out of my hand.

I don't wish to become embroiled in a rhubarb, but your beefing and stewing sound like sour grapes from a tough nut to crack—kind of like the pot calling the kettle black. But if you've digested the spoon-fed culinary metaphors from this meat-and-potatoes and bread-and-butter narrative, the rest will be gravy, duck soup, a picnic, a cream puff, a can of corn, a piece of cake, and easy as pie—just like taking candy from a baby.

Hot dog! I hope you're happy that this souped-up topic is a plum, not a lemon, the berries, not the pits. For all the tea in China, this cream of the crop of palate-pleasing food figures is bound to sell like hotcakes. I'm no glutton for punishment, but if I'm wrong, I'll eat crow and humble pie.

For my language comedy they pay me a whole lot of bread, dough, cabbage, clams, and lettuce—not small potatoes, chickenfeed, or peanuts. I've lived beyond my salad days to a ripe old age, but I'm also a smart cookie who's feeling his oats and who's full of beans. I may be wrinkled as a prune, but I'm a salt-of-the-earth good egg who takes the cake, knows his onions, makes life a bowl of cherries, and is the apple of your eye and the toast of the town. As always, the proof of the pudding is in the eating.

So in a nutshell, it all boils down to the fact that every day we say a mouthful, and we truly eat our words.

☺Unappetizing Menus

- A Japanese restaurant cautions, "Menus Are for Eating Customers Only."
- A Swiss restaurant boasts, "Our Wines Leave You Nothing to Hope For."
- An Indian restaurant advertises, "We Serve Tea In a Bag Like Mother."
- A Shanghai Mongolian hot-pot buffet guarantees, "You Will Be Able to Eat All You Wish Until You are Fed Up."
- An establishment in Cairo assures patrons that "The Drinking Water in This Restaurant Has Been Passed By The Authorities."

Hungry? Here's a "full-coarse meal" I've put together consisting of skewed and skewered items spotted by tourists around the world. Bon appetite!

Soup

Gritty Balloons in Soup

Barely Soup

Limpid Red Beet Soup
with Cheesy Dumplings
in the Form of a Finger

Fisherman's Crap Soup

Cup $5 / Bowel $8

Soap of the Day

Salad

Salad, a Firm's Own Make   Groin Salad
Thai Style Uterus Salad

Meat

Buff Steak   Gut Casserole
Warm Little Dogs   Hambugger
Calf Pluck   Dreaded Veel Cutlets
Roast Beast   Pork with Fresh Garbage
Sir Loin   Liver Worst
Meat Dumping   Demonic Steak
Irritable Scalloped Kidney Amiable and Sour Pork
Beef Rashers Beaten Up in the Country People's Fashion

Poultry

Chicken Low Mein   Frayed Chicken
Hen Fried with Butler   Goose Barnacles
Chicken in a Casket   Chicken Pox Pie
Foul Breast   Roasted Duck Let Loose
Utmost of Chicken Fried in Bother
Lightly Flowered Chicken Breast

Vegetables

Priest Fainted Eggplant   Muchrooms
Mushed Potatoes   Potato Cheeps
Cabitch

Sundries

Antipaste   Baked Zit
Toes with Butter & Jam   Mixed Boils to Pick
Fried Hormones   Muffled Frog Rumps

Fried Swarm   Gollum Shrimp
Spaghetti Fungoole   Drunken Prawns in Spit
         Tortilla Topped with Melted Cheese,
              Sour Cream, and Glaucoma

Desserts
Lady's Finger   Tart of the House
Strawberry Crap   Chocolate Mouse Tort
Chocolate Sand Kooky   Chocolate Puke

Beverages
White Whine   Turkey Coffee
         Special Cocktail for Women with Nuts

Taking Care of Business

ENGLISH MEANS BUSINESS

In bygone days, wandering peddlers were a familiar part of the American scene. An essential part of the peddlers' business was the buying and selling of gold. To test the value of gold, the peddler would file a shallow groove in the item he was considering and touch it with nitric acid. Color reactions from the acid would reveal the approximate gold content, and inferior metals would be decomposed by the treatment. This procedure was known as the *acid test*, and by extension, any exacting method designed to reveal hidden flaws has come to be known by this term.

Another golden word is *touchstone*, a criterion or standard, whose meaning goes straight back to goldsmiths, who kept hard stones, usually jasper or basalt, in their shops. When a customer brought in some gold, the goldsmith would rub it against the stone. With his practiced eye, the goldsmith could determine from the streak left on the stone the purity and quality of the gold. Hence, *touchstone*.

Business started out as a general term meaning literally "busyness." After several centuries of life, *business* picked up the narrower meaning of "commercial dealings." In 1925 Calvin Coolidge used the word in both its generalized an specialized senses when he stated, "The chief business of the American people is business." We today can see the word starting to generalize back to its first meaning in phrases like "I don't like this funny business one bit."

To the ledger of words once reserved for business alone we can add a number of products now shared in our common language:

I hope you feel that I'm *getting down to brass tacks* about business English. The popular explanation is that, in the past, dry goods stores, brass tacks were driven into the sales counters to mark a quarter-, half-, and full yard. Rather than holding up a bolt of piece goods and guessing the measurement, merchants would lay the swath on the counter and calculate accurately by *getting down to brass tacks*. Some language detectives lean toward *brass tacks* as cockney rhyming slang for *facts*.

Grocers of bygone days used a long pole or mechanical grabber (invented by Benjamin Franklin, by the way) to tip a can on a high shelf or at the top of a pile. The can would tumble into the grocer's waiting hands or open apron, just as a soft fly ball settles easily into a fielder's glove. That's why a languid fly ball in baseball is dubbed *a can of corn*.

In the days of hand typesetting, the terms *upper case* and *lower case* originated from the way that type—individual letters that were cast from metal alloys—were stored. The type was sorted by letter and kept in specially designed wooden or metal cases, with separate cases for capital and small letters. The case containing the capital letters—"the upper case"—was placed on a rack above the case housing the small, and more frequently used, letters—"the lower case."

Cliché comes to us from the Old French *cliquer*, "to click." That's the sound printers used to make when they took a wood engraving and struck it into molten lead to make a cast. This mold was a *stereotype,* from the Greek *stereos,* "solid," which was used to reproduce a picture over and over. Hence, the metaphorical stereotype, which forms a fixed, unchangeable image in the mind's eye.

Clichés begin their lives as imaginative expressions and comparisons. That's how they become clichés. Like a phonograph needle, our words settle into the grooves that the clichés have worn into our speech and writing. Phrases that once possessed power become trite, hackneyed, and lifeless—adjectives that themselves are clichés for clichés.

A student wrote in an essay, "The boy came back from recess with a cliché on his face."

"A cliché on his face? Whatever do you mean?" asked the teacher.

"A cliché!" the student answered. "You know, a worn-out expression."

Using clichés is as easy as ABC, one-two-three, pie, falling off a log, shooting fish in a barrel, and taking candy from a baby. They make us happy as a clam, a lark, a kid in a candy shop, and a pig in, uhm, slop.

But if you want to hit the bull's eye, the spot, the jackpot, the lottery, the ground running, the ball out of the park, and the nail on the head, then you should be able to avoid clichés like the plague.

Certain herbs sold in herbalists' shops were prepared ahead of time and thus lacked the freshness of herbs newly picked. Since the early eighteenth century, these herbs have been labeled *cut and dried.* It's easy to see how that phrase came to signify anything boring and lacking in spontaneity.

In the phrase *dead as a doornail,* what's so dead about a doornail? To find out, we must look back through the centuries to the craft of carpentry. Long-ago carpenters drove bigheaded metal nails into doors to connect the crosspieces on the back. The carpenters would hook the tip of the nail back to "clinch" the nail (as we clinch a deal). The nail was "dead," meaning "fixed, rigid, immovable," as in *deadline* and *deadlock.* Carpenters today still use the term "dead-nailing." It didn't take long for the pun on "fixed, rigid, immovable" and "not alive" to become clinched in our language, as in Charles Dickens's opening in *A Christmas Carol:* "Old Marley was as dead as a door-nail."

The noun *context* is borrowed from the Latin *contexere,* "to weave together." While many fabrics are colored or printed after they are woven, wool is sometimes dyed before it's woven into cloth. The color of that wool is through-and-through and impossible to remove completely. So when we say someone is a "dyed-in-the-wool" conservative, liberal, environmentalist, animal-rights supporter, Yankees fan, etc., we mean that their beliefs are steadfast and permanent.

Textiles are also woven into the word *spinster* (*spin* + *ster,* "woman who"), "a woman who spins cloth" and unhappily has come to designate "an older woman who remains unmarried." Mercifully, this word is dying out, along with the card game called Old Maid. Some spinsters worked with a distaff, a short staff that held a bundle of fibers, flax, or wool that were twisted into yarn or thread. Over time, *distaff* has become a figure of speech for "womankind." (The opposite of *distaff* is *sword side.*)

The adjective *normal* hails from Latin *normalis,* "a carpenter's square." This handy tool could ensure that your walls were at solid right angles and that all parts of a structure were even and balanced, i.e. *all squared away* and *on the level.*

Commercial life in medieval times was organized by guilds. An English apprentice who wished to be recognized as a master, with the right to work without supervision, was required to submit an article of metal, wood, stone, or leather, depending on his guild. Like today's academic dissertations, the quality of the work determined the artisan's future, and it came to be known as a *master piece.*

At one time, elaborate hats were a feature of everyday fashion. The people who made those hats were called hatters. They often used mercury to felt the animal fur they worked, but mercury had the side effect of making hatters go insane. The technical term for this illness is *erethism,* but the popular phrase is *mad as a hatter.*

When people say they feel they've been *put through the mill,* they echo a metaphor from the trade of milling. Grain fed to the jaws of a great stone mill is subjected to heavy and thorough grinding. By figurative extension, any person receiving rough treatment is said to be *put through the mill.* Related words and expressions include *milling around, run-of-the-mill,* and *millstone,* the circular stone used for grinding, but now meaning "a heavy burden."

I'll bet you've wondered what the heck is the whack that someone or something is out of in the vogue phrase *out of whack.* Wonder no more. The most likely source is the auctioneer's hammer, which, when whacked, signals the conclusion of a competitive purchase. Without that final whack, all is discombobulated, catawampus—out of whack. Out of *whack* bears some resemblance to *waiting for the other shoe to drop.* You're trying to fall asleep in a hotel room when you hear the thud of a shoe hitting the floor in the next room. You lie awake for hours waiting for the other shoe to drop.

FIGHTING WORDS

Knight is a word that has come up in the world. Descended from the Anglo-Saxon *cnicht* (sounded as two syllables), *knight* evolved from meaning "a boy" to "a servant," and, finally, "a servant of a noble." I am a freelance writer of magazine and newspaper pieces. That means that I write these articles on a fee-paid assignment basis rather than on a regular-salary basis for a single employer. Most medieval knights were committed to a feudal lord, but those who weren't could hire themselves and their lances to anyone willing to pay for their "freelance" military services. The word *freelance* is one of Sir Walter Scott's myriad word inventions, appearing first in his celebrated novel *Ivanhoe* (1820).

Writers, students, workers, and business people constantly face *deadlines*, dates when manuscripts homework, and reports must be submitted and orders filled. When such deadlines are not met, penalties result, such as lower grades or loss of business. But the punishment for passing beyond the original deadlines was more deadly.

During the American Civil War, a deadline was a line of demarcation around the inner stockade of a prison camp, generally about seventeen feet. At the notorious Confederate camp in Andersonville, Georgia, a line was actually marked out some distance from the outer wire fence. Any prisoner crossing this line was shot on sight.

Writer Douglas Adams quips, "I love deadlines. I like the whooshing sound they make as they fly by."

Most writers hope to create a *blockbuster*. That bombshell of a word originated in World War II Britain as Royal Air Force slang for a bomb of enough penetrating power to shatter whole blocks of homes and pavements. By the late 1940s *blockbuster* had come to signify a megahit play, film or book.

If adults commit adultery, do infants commit infantry? Chuckle chuckle, snort snort!—but we are led to ask what is the relationship, if any, between infants and *infantry? Infant* was born from the Latin *in-*, "not" + *fari*, "speak" = "one who is not yet capable of speech." In Italian, *infante* came to mean "boy" or "foot soldier"; hence, our word *infantry.*

A fancy synonym for the adjective *drunk* is *intoxicated.* The Greek word *toxon* meant "bow" (as in "arrow launcher"), and the poison Greek warriors used to tip their arrows took on the name *toxikon*. Thus, the first people to be intoxicated were those pierced by lethal arrows. Ultimately that poison became embedded in our word *intoxicate,* having traveled from the Greek military through late Latin *intoxicatus* to the drunken fellow who slurs, "Name your poison." Over time, *intoxicated* took on the figurative sense of "to excite or elate to the point of enthusiasm or frenzy."

War, humanity's most destructive enterprise, is also among its most productive when it comes to generating new language. Because warfare has been a depressingly constant feature of our history, many of our words, expressions, and metaphors are of bellicose descent. *Freelance, deadline,* and *blockbuster* are but three such words among thousands that have entered our language through warfare and other hostilities. Here march some more fighting words, ones that start with the letters *A* to *G:*

Ambulance issues from an invention of Napoleon Bonaparte's *l'hôpital ambulant* ("walking hospital"), a light litter that served as a field hospital for wounded soldiers. We see the word *amble* in the Preamble to our Constitution, an initial walk before the longer journey through the document.

Assassin descends from the Arabic *hashshashin,* literally "hashish eaters." The original hashshashin were members of a religious and military order located in the mountains of Lebanon. These fanatics would commit political murder after being intoxicated with great quantities of hashish.

During World War I, *AWOL,* meaning "Absent Without Official Leave," was pronounced as four distinct letters. During World War II, *AWOL* was sounded as a single word, and the meaning was extended to civilian life to identify any person absent from any job or activity without explanation.

The 1960s expression *bang for the buck* began as a frivolous iteration for how much destructive power the Defense Department gets for the money it pays.

Figuratively, a *battle-ax* is a pejorative expression for a woman, often elderly, who is unpleasantly loud and aggressive. The original battle-ax was a sharp, broad ax used by Gothic tribes. When wielded or thrown, the weapon could penetrate Roman armor and split a shield

Visit a Revolutionary War battle site such as Fort Ticonderoga, and you may see some gruesome artifacts in its museum—bullets with teeth marks in them. Possessing no real anesthesia to ease the agony of amputation, long-ago surgeons offered wounded soldiers the only pain reducer they could—a bullet to bite hard on. Just thinking about such trauma is enough to make me *sweat bullets*. After anesthesia was introduced in the United States in 1844, the expression *bite the bullet* came figuratively to mean "to deal with a stressful situation resolutely," as in Rudyard Kipling's lines:

> Bite the bullet, old man,
> And don't let them think you're afraid.

After the Norman Conquest of England in A.D. 1066, William the Conqueror required civilians to extinguish all fires and candles and stay inside after dark. Night patrols enforced this regulation by calling out "*Couvre feu!*" ("cover the fire"), which became *curfew* in English.

A *cohort* was a Roman military unit, composed of one tenth of a Roman legion.

An *emeritus* was originally a Roman soldier who had completed his term of service (Latin *emereor,* "obtain by service") and earned his discharge. Nowadays emeritus refers to retired professors, clergymen, and other retired officials.

A flash in the pan sounds as if it derives from the way prospectors pan rivers for gold. In truth, though, *a flash in the pan* refers to the occasional misfiring of the old flintlock muskets when the flash of the primer in the pan of the rifle failed to ignite the explosion of the charge. It is estimated that such misfirings ran as high as fifteen percent, leading *a flash in the pan* to come to mean "an intense but short-lived success or a person who fails to live up to their early promise."

Since the eighteenth century *field day* has designated a special day set aside for military maneuvers and reviews.

Through a linguistic process called expansion, *field day* has broadened to mean "a day marked by a sense of occasion and great success."

Muzzle loaders, then as now, had a half cock, or safety position, for a gun's hammer that back-locked the trigger mechanism so that the weapon couldn't be fired. The half-cock position doesn't generate enough power to make sparks to fire the pistol, so when a person *goes off half-cocked*, they are not in control of the situation.

The theory you've most likely heard that explains the birth of *gringo* is that U.S. troops marching off to the Mexican-American War (1846–48) lustily sang, "Green Grow the Rushes-O," prompting the Mexicans to construct *gringo* from the first two words of the title. In truth, *gringo* inhabited the Spanish vocabulary since the early eighteenth century, long before the Mexican-American conflict. Just as we say, "It's all Greek to me," Spanish speakers said, *hablar en griego,* "to speak in Greek," meaning "to speak in an unintelligible foreign tongue." It didn't take long for *griego* to morph into *gringo.*

WHAT'S MY LINE?

The verb *to vet* means "to examine credentials, manuscripts, or other documents as a veterinarian examines an animal, hoping to give it a clean bill of health." The noun *veterinarian* came about because the first veterinarians treated only animals that were old (Latin *vetus*) and experienced enough to perform work such as pulling a plow or hauling military baggage. That's why *veteran* and *veterinarian* start with almost the same letters.

Most occupational titles are self-explanatory: A teacher teaches, a preacher preaches, a gardener gardens, and a writer writes. But the origins of some job names are more obscure. *Veterinarian* is one example. *Janitor* is another, deriving from the Roman god Janus, who guarded doorways. A *professor* is "one who makes public declarations," while the first *deans* were military officers in charge of ten (*decem*) soldiers. Those *soldiers* were so called because they were paid in Roman coins called *solidi.*

A ventriloquist is someone who is skilled in the art of throwing his or her voice so that it appears to emanate from a source other than the speaker. Appropriately, the roots of *ventriloquist* are the Latin *ventris*, "belly" + *loqui,* "speaker." In other words, a ventriloquist is a "belly speaker." (I'm thinking of one day writing a book titled *Ventriloquism For Dummies.*)

The standard explanation traces *cop* or *copper*, meaning "police," to copper buttons worn on early police uniforms, or to copper police badges supposedly issued in some cities, but there is no convincing evidence for this conjecture.

Another theory explains *cop* as an acronym standing for "constable on patrol" or "chief of police." But these acronymic etymologies almost always turn out to be spurious, after-the-fact explanations. Another inconvenient truth is that acronyms were virtually unknown in English before the twentieth century, while *cop* itself was well-established by the mid-nineteenth century.

In reality, the law enforcement sense of *cop* and *copper* harks back to the Latin word *capere,* meaning "to seize," which also gives us *capture. Cop* as a slang term meaning "to catch, snatch, or grab" took its place in English in the eighteenth century. Criminals apprehended by the police were said to have been "copped"—caught by the "coppers" or "cops."

Why are psychiatrists often called shrinks? After all, psychiatry seeks to expand people's self-knowledge, abilities, and options, not to shrink them. Turns out that the slang term *shrink* applied to those who practice psychotherapy is a shortened form of *headshrinker,* a jocular comparison to primitive peoples who dry and *shrink* the heads of their slain enemies. The first print occurrence of shrink used in this way reposes in Thomas Pynchon's 1967 novel, *The Crying of Lot 49.*

When Geoffrey Chaucer quilled in his Prologue to *The Canterbury Tales*, "a clerk ther was of Oxenford," the poet was referring to a clergyman or cleric, the first meaning of the word *clerk*. In the Middle Ages, literacy was largely confined to the clergy, but *clerk* gradually became the name for bookkeepers, secretaries, and notaries—anyone who could read or write.

Now have a look at a passage from *The Octopus* (1901), by American novelist Frank Norris:

> Lyman Derrick sat dictating letters to his typewriter. "That's all for the present," he said at length. Without reply, the typewriter rose and withdrew, thrusting her pencil into the coil of her hair, closing the door behind her, softly, discreetly.

Norris was not fabricating a science-fiction tale featuring robot typewriters. Rather, back in the late nineteenth and early twentieth century, a typewriter was a person who worked on a typewriting machine, not the machine itself.

Have you ever worried about the fact that the person with whom you trust your hard-earned life savings is called a *broker*? Worry no more: The original broker was one who broaches (opens) casks of wine.

The word *usher* has a long history, going all the way back to the Latin *ostium,* "door," related to *os,* "mouth," because a door was likened to the mouth of a building. *Usher*, then, turns out to be a body metaphor for a person who stands at a door.

The surname *Webber* means "a man who weaves," *Webster* "a woman who weaves." *Brewer* signifies "a man who brews," *Brewster* "a woman who brews." *Dyer* is the last name of "a man who dyes cloth," *Dexter* the last name of "a woman who dyes cloth." *Baker,* of course, denotes "a man who bakes," while *Baxter* denotes "a woman who bakes."

Here's an inventory of additional vocational names and their not-so-apparent origins:

- *bursar.* one who controls the purse (*bursa*)
- *chauffeur.* one who stokes the fires of the engine in a steam-driven car
- *constable.* one who tended his lord's horses and stables
- *coroner.* an officer of the crown (*corona*)
- *diplomat.* one who vets and carries an official state document (related to *diploma*)
- *grocer.* one who sells by the gross
- *manufacturer.* one who makes products by hand (Latin *manus*, "hand" + *facere*, "perform.")
- *nurse.* one who nourishes
- *orthopedist.* one who corrects (the bones of) children
- *pastor.* a spiritual herdsman
- *plumber.* one who works with lead (*plumbum*)
- *restaurateur.* one who works at a place where patrons are restored
- *secretary.* one to whom secrets are entrusted
- *sheriff.* a stitching together of Old English *shire*, "county," and *reeve*, "local administrator"
- *surgeon.* one who works with his hands
- *vicar.* substitute for God (*vicarious*).
- *whitesmith.* A blacksmith forges iron; a whitesmith works with tin.

COINING PHRASES

Money makes the world go around. It also makes our language go around. Not only does money talk. We talk about money.

To coin a phrase, I'm not a guy who's phony as a three dollar bill and not worth a red cent or a plugged nickel. I'm not penny wise and pound foolish, and I won't short change you. Dollars to doughnuts, I'm not a day late and a dollar short, and I won't nickel and dime you to death. If you don't give me your two cents, I'll give you a penny for your thoughts.

We also make jokes about money:

- You look like a million dollars—all green and wrinkled.
- Have you heard about the couple who spent $250,000 on their son's college education—and all they got was a quarterback?
- Do you want to get rich? Simply purchase fifty female pigs and fifty male deer—and you'll have a hundred sows and bucks.

Now I'm going to put my money where my mouth is. I'm also going to put my mouth where the money is. That's why they pay me the big bucks.

Most of us consider a talent to be a gift that has little to do with money. But in ancient times a talent was a unit of weight in silver or gold that functioned as a monetary unit, one that figures prominently in Jesus's parable of the talents (Matthew 25: 14-15): "For the kingdom of heaven is as a man traveling in a far country, who called his own servants and delivered unto them his goods. And unto one he gave five talents, to another two and to another one, to every man according to his several ability." The current meaning of *talent*, some special, often God-given ability or aptitude, is a figurative extension of the parable.

We strive *to make ends meet*. What are the ends, and how do they meet? The phrase was originally a nineteenth-century bookkeeping term. The bookkeeper's task was, and still is, to make both ends ("assets and liabilities") mete ("equal, balance"). There's no accounting for taste, and, as for me, I have no taste for accounting.

What about the ubiquitous financial metaphor *scot-free*? The compound has nothing to do with Scotland or the Scottish people. Even before Shakespeare's day, a scot was a municipal tax paid to a sheriff or bailiff. So for centuries those who got off scot-free managed to avoid paying their taxes. Their progeny still walk the earth.

A *picayune* was originally a Spanish half real (pronounced "ray-ahl") worth about six cents and circulated throughout the American South. It didn't take long for prices to rise and for inflation to erode the already paltry value of the coin. Up grew the phrase "not worth a picayune," referring to something of little value. Before long, *to be picayune* about a matter came to mean to be petty or picky.

Here's a quiz that's right on the money. Fill in each blank with a monetary term.

1. Don't take any wooden _____.
2. Two bits, four bits, six bits, a _____!
3. Don't pass the _____.
4. You can bet your bottom _____.
5. Turn on a _____.
6. My stamp collection is in _____ condition.

The answers are *nickels, dollar, buck, dollar, dime,* and *mint.* Whence the wooden nickel in the first poser? During the centennial celebration of the United States, in Philadelphia, commemorative tokens made of wood sold for five cents each. These coins were accepted as legal tender while the festivities were in progress; but, of course, they ceased to have value after the show was over. So beginning in the last part of the nineteenth century, the advice *Don't take any wooden nickels* became the popular equivalent of "Don't be a sucker."

Regarding the second question, why do two bits equal a quarter, four bits a half dollar, and six bits seventy-five cents? Because early in our nation's history, Mexican currency was used interchangeably with local coinage, and the Spanish real ("re-AHL"), a coin worth twelve- and-a-half cents, was called a bit. When the U.S. quarter dollar piece was minted, it quickly acquired the slang label *two bits.*

You can *bank on* my expertise; *it's like money in the bank,* and *you can take it to the bank.* No longer will you be unable *to make head nor tail* of monetary expressions.

☺You're Fired!

The meaning of *fired*, "to discharge someone from a job," is an extension of applying fire to gunpowder. But nobody gets fired anymore. How do I fire thee? Let me count the ways. Euphemisms for getting bounced include *decruited, deselected, destaffed, downsized, excessed, indefinite idling, negotiated departure, nonpositively terminated, nonretained, outplaced, premature retirement, reclassified, redundancy elimination, RIF (reduction in force), vocational relocation, involuntary normal attrition*, and (gasp!) *workforce imbalance correction*.

I powerfully doubt that such corporate doublespeak assuages the workers, who knew they are really being *fired, axed, bounced, canned, eighty-sixed, laid off, let go, sacked, shown the door*, and *given the old heave-ho*.

In the continuing search for newer, softer, and more ambiguous verbs with which to administer the final blow to helpless jobholders, Laurence Urdang, the late editor of the late *Verbatim, the Language Quarterly*, came up with a sparkling new pun game:

If clergymen are defrocked and lawyers are disbarred, then alcoholics are delivered, hairdressers are distressed, manicurists are defiled, models are disposed, and pornographers are deluded.

Employing the *de-* and *dis-* prefixes, I offer my own multiple verbs for getting rid of members of other professions:

- Bankers are distrusted and disinterested.
- Cowboys are debunked, deranged, and decaffeinated.
- Elks Clubbers are dislodged and dismembered.
- Judges are disrobed, dishonored, disappointed, and defined.
- Magicians are dispelled and disillusioned.
- Mathematicians are deciphered, disfigured, discounted, and dissolved.
- Preachers are demoralized, decreed, distracted, and dissected.
- Songwriters are denoted and decomposed.
- Tailors are depressed, depleted, and dispatched.
- Teachers are declassified, detested, and degraded.
- Tennis players are deduced, disadvantaged, deserved, and defaulted.

☺NOTHING WORKS FOR ME

Some people hold the same job for their entire career. Others move from one job to another while relentlessly ascending the corporate ladder. My personal workplace history is more checkered:

- My first job was working in an orange juice factory, but I couldn't concentrate, so I got canned.
- Then I became a lumberjack, but I just couldn't hack it, so they gave me the axe.
- I was once a set designer, but I left without making a scene.
- I was next employed at a diet center, but I got downsized.
- I became a baker, but I turned out to be a loafer and couldn't make enough dough.
- Then I opened a donut shop, but I soon got tired of the hole business.
- I manufactured calendars, but my days were numbered.
- After that I tried to be a tailor, but I just wasn't suited for it, mainly because it was a sew-sew job, de-pleating, and de-pressing.
- I took a job as an upholsterer, but I never recovered.
- Next I worked in a muffler factory, but that was exhausting.

- I became a hairdresser, but the job was just too cut-and-dried.
- I moved on to selling lingerie, but they decided to give me a pink slip.
- I tried telemarketing, but I had too many hang-ups.
- I manned a computer but developed a terminal illness and lost my drive and my memory.
- I became a dentist, but gummed up the works and couldn't do the drill. The job was boring and felt like a bridge to nowhere.
- I worked as a fortune-teller, but I didn't see any future in it.
- I sold origami, but the business folded.
- For a while, I was an astrologer, but it wasn't in the stars.
- Then I tried to be a chef. I figured it would add a little spice to my life, but I just didn't have the thyme, it didn't pan out, and my goose was cooked.
- I attempted to be a deli worker, but any way I sliced it, I couldn't cut the mustard.
- I studied a long time to become a doctor, but I didn't have the patients.
- I became a cardiologist, but my heart just wasn't in it.
- I took a job at UPS, but I couldn't express myself.
- Next was a job in a shoe factory, but the job didn't last and I got the boot.
- I studied to become a lawyer, but my career was brief. It was too trying and had no appeal.
- I tried selling vacuum cleaners, but the job really sucked.
- I became a Velcro salesman but couldn't stick with it.

- I was a commercial fisherman, but I missed the boat and discovered that I couldn't tackle the job and live on my net income.
- I was a masseur for a while, but I rubbed people the wrong way.
- I was once a photographer, but I never developed. It was a negative experience, and I hated the hot flashes.
- I became a Hawaiian garland maker, but I got leid off.
- So I turned to designing lingerie, but I got the pink slip.
- I was a printer for a while, but I wasn't the type for the job, and I didn't have an inkling about what to do.
- I tried being a fireman, but I suffered burnout, so I couldn't climb my way to the top.
- I wanted to be a banker, but I wasn't ready to make a change. I lacked interest and maturity so I withdrew from consideration.
- I got a job at a zoo feeding giraffes, but I was fired because I wasn't up to it.
- So then I became a personal trainer in a gym, but they said I wasn't fit for the job.
- I tried selling cigarette lighters, but I lost my spark.
- Next, I found being an electrician interesting, but I had to strip to make ends meet. I wasn't emotionally grounded and the work was shocking and revolting, so they discharged me.
- I thought that becoming a tennis pro would yield a net gain, but it wasn't my kind of racket. I was too high-strung and didn't have any love for the game.

- I tried being a teacher, but I soon lost my principal, my faculties, and my class.
- I trained to be a ballet dancer, but I was seldom on point and it was too-too difficult.
- For a while, I was a farmer, but problems cropped up and I wasn't outstanding in my field.
- I took the plunge as a plumber, but it turned out to be a pipe dream. I was out of sink, so the job went down the drain.
- I worked as an elevator operator. The job had its ups and downs. I got the shaft and took steps to quit.
- I applied for a job at an Air & Space Museum, but there was nothing inside.
- I thought about becoming a poet, but the work was a verse to my being. Iamb what iamb.
- I sold chocolate ice cream, diced marshmallows, and nuts, but the job became a rocky road.
- I became a candle maker. At first business waxed strong. Then it tapered off.
- My first day on the snow job as a ski instructor I slipped up, and it was all downhill from there.
- I did a stint at a pizza place. I kneaded the dough, but my pies were cheesy.
- I took a job as a cook in a monastery as both the fish friar and the chip monk. I tried to communicate with the clergy, but they excommunicated me.
- I once worked as an optometrist. The future looked clear, and my life was coming into focus. Then I got too close to the lens grinder and made a spectacle of myself.

- I tried cleaning pools, but I went into the tank and was out of my depth.
- I became a statistician, but I got broken down by age, sex, and marital status.
- I was once a Scrabble champion, but I became inconsonant, and I can't move my vowels anymore.

So I've retired, and I find that I'm perfect for this job!

HATS IN THE RING

A Primer of Political Words

Although the classical societies of ancient Greece and Rome have vanished, Greek and Roman thought is very much alive in the parlance of politics. As the joke goes, the etymology of the word *politics* derives from *poly*, "many," and *tics*, which are blood-sucking parasites. In truth, *politics* issues from the Greek word *polities*, "city, citizen." Politics may make strange bedfellows, but, as we shall see, politics makes for even stranger, and sometimes colorful, vocabulary.

Taking first things first, I'll start with the word *primary*, which descends from the Latin *primus*, "first." *Primary*, as a shortening of "primary election, is first recorded in 1861. In an *election* we "pick out" a candidate whom we wish to vote for. In Latin *e* means "out" and *lectus* "pick or choose."

Campaign is very much a fighting word. The Latin *campus*, "field," is a clue that the first campaigns were conducted on battlefields. A military campaign is a series of operations mounted to achieve a particular wartime objective. A political campaign is an all-out effort to secure the election of a candidate to office.

When he went to the Forum in Roman times, a *candidate* for office wore a bleached white toga to symbolize his humility, purity of motive and candor. The original Latin root, *candidatus*, meant "one who wears white," from the belief that white was the color of purity and probity. There was wishful thinking even in ancient Roman politics, even though a white-clad

Roman *candidatus* was accompanied by *sectatores*, followers who helped him get votes by bargaining and bribery. The Latin parent verb *candere*, "to shine, to glow" can be recognized in the English words *candid, candor, candle, chandelier,* and *incandescent.*

We know that candidates are ambitious; it's also worth knowing that *ambition* developed from the Latin *ambitionem*, "a going about," from the going about of candidates for office in ancient Rome.

President descends from the Latin *praesidio*, "preside, sit in front of or protect." Presidents sit in the seat of government. When we speak of "the ship of state," we are being more accurate etymologically than we know. The Greek word *kybernao* meant "to direct a ship." The Romans borrowed the word as *guberno*, and ultimately it crossed the English Channel as *governor*, originally a steersman. That's why the noun is *governor* and the adjective *gubernatorial.*

The story behind the word *inaugurate* is an intriguing one. The word literally means "to take omens from the flight of birds." In ancient Rome, augurs would predict the outcome of an enterprise by the way the birds were flying. "To auger well" means "to prophesy favorably." Augurs (the first "early birders") were also known as auspices, whence our word *auspicious*, from the Latin *avis*, "bird" + *specere*, "to observe."

These soothsayers, magicians, and priests would tell a general whether to march or to do battle by the formations of the birds on the wing. They might even catch one and cut it open to observe its entrails for omens. Nowadays, presidential candidates use their inauguration speeches to take flight on an updraft of words, rather than birds—and they often spill their guts for all to see.

Filibuster is imported from the Dutch *vrijbuiter,* "freeboo-ter," which first meant "pirate, adventurer, one who plunders freely" in English. That sense is retained in the current deno-tation of *filibuster:* "holding a piece of legislation captive by making long and windy speeches."

The verb *to ostracize* means "to exclude from a group by popular consent," and hidden in that verb is an oyster. Rather than clamming up and floundering, just for the halibut let's go fishing for the origin of *ostracize.* Oysters were a staple of the ancient Greek diet, and the verb *to ostracize* descends directly from *ostrakon,* the Greek word for an oyster shell and also for a broken piece of pottery. In ancient Athens, the people could banish a politician by popular vote. Citizens gathered in the market place and wrote down the name of the undesirable on a tile or potsherd. If enough votes were dropped into an urn, the "winner" was sent from the city for either five or ten years. Because the shards of pottery resembled oyster shells, they were called *ostrakon,* whence our verb for general exclusion.

Centuries after the *ostrakon,* Italians used small balls or pebbles to vote, "casting" them into one box or another. Hence, the word *ballot,* "a small ball or pebble." If a majority of black balls were placed in a ballot box, the candidate was *blackballed,* "excluded, ostracized."

The original Greek meaning of the word *idiot* was not a matter of I.Q. Long before the psychologists got hold of the word, the Greeks used *idiotes,* from the root *idios,* "private," as in *idiom* and *idiosyncrasy,* to designate those who did not hold public office. Because such people possessed no special status or skill, the word *idiot* gradually fell into disrepute.

The *vote* that responsible citizens cast is really a "vow" or "wish." And this is the precise meaning of the Latin *votum.*

People in our society who fail to exercise their democratic privilege of voting on election day are sometimes called idiots.

The political expression "to throw one's hat in the ring" probably derives from the custom of tossing one's hat into the boxing ring to signal the acceptance of a pugilist's challenge. Once the hat is thrown, the candidates start engaging in political infighting as they slug it out with their opponents.

During the nineteenth century, a dedicated follower showed support for a political candidate by carrying a torch in an evening campaign parade. A fellow who "carried a torch" in such a rally didn't care who knew that he was wholeheartedly behind his candidate. Later the term was applied to someone publicly (and obsessively) in love.

One more metaphor that was originally literal attaches to bandwagons, high wagons large enough to hold a band of musicians. Early bandwagons were horse-drawn through the streets in order to publicize an upcoming event. Political candidates would ride a bandwagon through a town, and those who wished to show their support would "hop [or climb] on the bandwagon" and ride with the candidate and his blaring band.

Horses and horse racing are dominant animal metaphors that gallop through political life. One of the earliest of equine metaphors is "dark horse." The figure refers to a political candidate who is nominated unexpectedly, usually as a result of compromise between two factions in a party. Dark horse candidates who became president include James Polk in 1844, Franklin Pierce in 1852, Rutherford B. Hayes in 1876, James Garfield in 1880, and Warren G. Harding in 1920.

Presidents always have running mates. This too is a horse racing term and derives from the practice of one owner or one stable running two horses in a race, the slower one being put in there to pace the star. The pacesetter was known as the star's running mate. The phrase has been around for more than a century, but its use to define a vice president was coined by, of all non-practitioners of slang, the most scholarly, the most ecclesiastical of presidents, Woodrow Wilson. At the Democratic Convention in 1912 the presidential nomination went to Wilson on the forty-sixth ballot after a terrific brawl. Governor Wilson of New Jersey announced that his vice presidential choice would be another governor, Thomas Marshall, and announced, "And I feel honored by having him as my running mate." Wilson's turn of phrase brought the house down, the only squeak of humor those assembled had ever heard out of Woodrow Wilson.

Presidential jockeying for position gets out of the gate earlier and earlier with each campaign. It remains to be seen whether the next presidential contest will turn out to be a runaway or a real horse race. Will a dark horse give the front-runner a run for his or her money? Will the old war horse and his or her running mate, saddled with international and economic problems, turn out to be shoo-ins or lame ducks?

OK!

Explanations for the origin of *OK* have been as imaginative as they have been various. But Professor Alan Walker Read, a professor at Columbia University, proved that *OK* did not derive from *okeh,* an affirmative reply in Choctaw; nor from the name of chief Old Keokuk; nor from a fellow named Orrin Kendall, who manufactured a tasty brand of army biscuit for Union soldiers in the Civil War; nor from the Haitian port Aux Cayes, which produced superior rum; nor from "open key," a telegraph term; nor from the Greek *olla kalla,* "all good."

Professor Read demonstrated that *OK* started life as an obscure joke and through a twist of fate went to the top of the charts on the American hit parade of words. In the 1830s, in New England, there was a craze for initialisms, in the manner of *FYI, LOL,* OMG, and *TGIF,* so popular today. The fad went so far as to generate letter combinations of intentionally comic misspellings: *KG* for "know go," *KY* for "know yuse," *NSMJ* for "'nough said 'mong jentlemen," and *OR* for "oll wrong." *OK* for "oll korrect" naturally followed.

Of all those loopy initialisms and facetious misspellings, *OK* alone survived. That's because of a presidential nickname that consolidated the letters in the national memory. Martin Van Buren, elected our eighth president in 1836, was born in Kinderhook, New York, and, early in his political career, was dubbed "Old Kinderhook." Echoing the "Oll Korrect" initialism, *OK* became the rallying cry of the Old Kinderhook Club, a Democratic organization supporting Van Buren during the 1840 campaign. Thus, the accident of Van Buren's birthplace rescued *OK* from the dustbin of history.

The coinage did Van Buren no good. He was defeated in his bid for re-election. But the word honoring the name of his birthplace today remains what H. L. Mencken identified as "the most shining and successful Americanism ever invented."

TEDDY'S BEAR

Mothers sewed stuffed bears before President Theodore Roosevelt came along, but no one called them teddy bears. Not until November 1902, when Roosevelt traveled to Smedes, Mississippi, where he was acting as adjudicator for a border dispute between Louisiana and Mississippi.

On November 14, during a break in the negotiations, Roosevelt was invited by southern friends to go bear hunting. He felt that he could consolidate his support in the South by appearing there in the relaxed atmosphere of a hunting party, so he accepted the invitation.

During the hunt, Roosevelt's hosts cornered a bear cub, and a guide roped it to a tree for the president to kill. Roosevelt declined to shoot the cub, believing such an act to be beneath his dignity as a hunter and as a man: "If I shot that little fellow, I wouldn't be able to look my boys in the face again."

That Sunday's *Washington Post* carried a cartoon, drawn by artist Clifford Berryman. T.R. stood in hunting gear, rifle in hand and his back toward the cowering cub. The caption read, "Drawing the line in Mississippi," referring both to the border dispute and to animal ethics.

Now the story switches to the wilds of Brooklyn, N.Y. There Russian immigrants Morris and Rose Michtom owned a candy store where they sold refreshments, novelties, and toys, including handmade stuffed animals. Inspired by Berryman's cartoon, Rose Michtom made a toy bear and displayed it in the shop window. The bear proved popular with the public.

The Michtoms sent President Roosevelt the very bear they had put in their window. They said it was meant for Roosevelt's grandchildren and asked T.R. for permission to name the bear after him. The president replied, "I don't know what my name may mean to the bear business, but you're welcome to use it."

Well, T.R.'s name turned out to do a lot for the bear business. Rose and Morris began turning out stuffed cubs labeled *Teddy's bear,* in honor of our twenty-sixth president, and business boomed. As the demand increased, the family hired extra seamstresses and rented a warehouse. Their operation eventually became the Ideal Toy Corporation.

The bear was a prominent emblem in Roosevelt's successful 1904 election campaign, and *Teddy's bear* was enshrined in dictionaries in 1907. Cartoonist Berryman never sought compensation for the use of the cub he had created. He simply smiled and said, "I have made thousands of children happy. That is enough for me."

☺ POLITICAL TICKLES

More than 2,500 years ago, the fabulist Aesop observed, "We hang the petty thieves and appoint the great ones to public office." Ambrose Bierce sardonically defined *politics* as "A strife of interest masquerading as a contest of principles." Robert Louis Stevenson noted that "politics is perhaps the only profession for which no preparation is thought necessary." President Ronald Reagan quipped, "Politics is supposed to be the second oldest profession. I have come to realize that it bears a very close resemblance to the first." H. L. Mencken defined a politician as "a man who will double-cross that bridge when he comes to it."

That's the same H. L. Mencken who observed, "Under democracy, one party always devotes its chief energies to trying to prove that the other party is unfit to rule—and both commonly succeed, and are right." Mencken's contemporary, Clarence Darrow, echoed that sentiment: "When I was a boy I was told that anybody could become President. Now I'm beginning to believe it."

In support of Darrow's point, remember that Jefferson did it, Nixon did it, and Truman did it. So any Tom, Dick, and Harry can become President of the United States!

Have you ever wondered: If *pro* and *con* are opposites, is congress the opposite of progress? Mark Twain loved to pick on members of Congress: "No man's life, liberty, or property are safe while the legislature is in session," he declared, as well as "Talk is cheap, except when Congress does it" and "It could probably be shown by facts and figures that there is no distinctly native American criminal class, except Congress." His sharpest congressional barb goes like this: "Suppose you were an idiot. And suppose you were a member of Congress. But I repeat myself."

Politicians have been riddled by riddles:

- What do we call voting in America? *Electile Dysfunction.*
- How can you tell when a politician is lying? *His lips are moving.*
- Have you heard about the new dance called The Politician? *You take three steps forward, two steps backward, then side-step, side-step, and reverse direction.*
- What do politicians and diapers have in common? *They both need changing regularly—and for the same reason.*
- Why should all politicians wear uniforms, like NASCAR drivers? *So we can identify their corporate sponsors.*

Political jokes can be very powerful. That's why so many of them get elected. Will Rogers explained, "I don't make jokes. I just watch the government and report the facts." Jay Leno observed, "If God wanted us to vote, he would have given us candidates."

That's why *political science* is an oxymoron.

☺AMERICAN HISTORY ACCORDING TO STUDENT BLOOPERS

It is truly astounding what havoc students can wreak upon the chronicles of the human race. I have pasted together the following "history" of the world from genuine, certified, authentic student bloopers collected from teachers throughout the world, from eighth grade through college level.

Read carefully, and you will learn a lot.

Christopher Columbus was a great navigator who discovered America while cursing about the Atlantic Ocean on the Nina, the Pinta Colada, and the Santa Fe.

Later, Jamestown was discovered by King James the One and named after him. The Pilgrims drove the Mayflower across the ocean and arrived in hardships. This was called the Pill's Grim Progress. These people always wore old shoes with a big buckle on the top of them. The men wore pants that only came a little ways past their knees, and the girls wore funny bonnets.

The winter of 1620 was a hard one for the settlers. Many people died, and many babies were born. Captain John Smith was responsible for all this.

One of the causes of the Revolutionary War was the English put tacks in their tea. The Boston Tea Party was a raid where they threw all the tea into Boston Harbor, which they all drank. Finally, General Corn Wallace surrendered and the War was over. When General Burgundy surrendered to Sara's Toga, the colonists won the war and no longer had to pay for taxis.

America was founded by four fathers. Delegates from the original thirteen states formed the Contented Congress. Thomas Jefferson, a Virgin, and Benjamin Franklin were two singers of the Decoration of Independence, which says that all men are cremated equal and are well endowed by their creator.

Benjamin Franklin had gone to Boston carrying all his clothes in his pocket and a loaf of bread under each arm. He invented electricity by rubbing two cats backwards and declared, "A horse divided against itself cannot stand." Franklin died in 1790 and is still dead.

George Washington crossed the Delaware River, married Martha Custis, and in due time became the Father of Our Country. The difference between a king and a president is that a king is the son of his father, but a president isn't. Washington's farewell address was Mount Vernon.

Soon the Constitution of the United States was adopted to secure domestic hostility. Under the Constitution, the people have the right to bare arms.

In the early nineteenth century, Lois and Clark explored the Louisiana Purchase. The two greatest marshals of the Old West were Wyatt Burp and Wild Bill Hiccup. General George Custard extinguished himself at the Battle of the Little Big Horn.

Abraham Lincoln became America's greatest Precedent. Lincoln's mother died in infancy, and he was born in a log cabin which he built with his very own hands. When Lincoln was president, he wore only a tall silk hat. He said,

"In onion there is strength." Lincoln wrote the Emasculation Proclamation, and he kept our country in one peace. His last residence was at the Gettysburg Address. Lincoln wrote the Gettysburg Address while traveling from Washington to Gettysburg on the back of an envelope.

On the night of April 14, 1865, Lincoln went to the theater and got shot in his seat by one of the actors in a moving picture show. The believed assinator was John Wilkes Booth, a supposingly insane actor. This ruined Booth's career.

During the Industrial Revolution, people stopped reproducing by hand and started reproducing by machine. The invention of the steamboat by Robert Fulton caused a network of rivers to spring up. Samuel Morse invented a code of telepathy. Eli Whitney invented the spinning gin. Thomas Edison invented the pornograph and the indecent lamp. Andrew Carnegie started the steal business. And George Goethals dug the alimentary canal.

The First World War was caused by the assignation of the Arch-Duck by an anahist.

Charles Limburger was the first man to ever cross the Atlantic alone. He wanted to go by regular airlines, but he couldn't afford to buy a ticket. When he got to Paris, all the French people shouted, "Bonsai!"

World War II happened when Adolph Hitler and the Knotsies had erotic dreams of conquest all over Europe. Wilt Chamberlain practiced appeasement in Europe before the Second World War. Franklin Roosevelt put a stop to Hitler, who committed suicide in his bunk.

Martin Luther had a dream. He went to Washington and recited his Sermon on the Monument. Later, he nailed ninety-six Protestants in the Watergate Scandal, which ushered in a new error in the anals of human history.

SACRED WORDS

THAT OLD-TIME RELIGION

We think of carnivals as traveling entertainments with rides, sideshows, games, cotton candy, and balloons. But the first carnivals were pre-Lenten celebrations—a last fling before penitence. The Latin word parts *carne*, "meat, flesh," and *vale*, "farewell," indicate that the earliest carnivals were seasons of feasting and merrymaking, "a farewell to meat" just before Lent.

Why can *story* mean both "a tale" and "the level of a building"? Both words come down to us from the Latin *historia*, "to know," and French *histoire*, where it means both "a tale" and "history." The endurance of the meanings "tale" and "floor" is architectural. Back in the Middle Ages, it was the custom in many parts of Europe to paint scenes depicting historical, legendary, biblical, or literary subjects on the outside of the various floors of buildings. Each level represented a story, and, before long, the levels themselves were called stories.

Religion, derived from the Latin *religionem,* "respect for what is sacred," "to bind fast," binds people together and with God or gods and influences a great many lives and the words we speak and hear and write and read every day. *Story* is one of many words and expressions that began in religion. Because our society has become secularized, we overlook the religious foundation of our daily parlance:

The literal meaning of *atone* issues from what the word actually looks like—to be "at one," that is, united with God.

Bonfires were originally the bone fires that consumed the bodies of saints who were burned during the English Reformation.

Enthusiastic, from the Greek *enthusiasmos,* "a god within," first meant "filled with God," as did *giddy,* from Anglo Saxon *gydig,* "god-held man."

The Latin word for "cross," *crux,* is embedded in the words *crux, crucial, cruise, crusade,* and *excruciating,* which has broadened from denoting the agony of the crucifixion to any kind of torturous pain.

Fan, is a clipping of *fanatic,* from the Latin *fanaticus,* "inspired by the temple." The opposite, *profane,* describes a person who is irreverent, from the Latin *pro,* "outside," and *fanum,* "the temple."

Our traditional farewell, *good-bye,* turns out to be a shortening of the sentence "God be with you."

In its original meaning, an *icon* was a small religious painting used as an aid to devotion. In its new meaning, icons are now people who achieve superstar status in the worlds of politics, sports, the arts and entertainment. Many consider this change to be a debasement of a perfectly good word.

A *red-letter day* is so- called because of the practice of calendar and almanac publishers of printing the numbers of saints' days and religious feast days in red ink. Such days now describe any distinctive day in a person's life, such as birthdays, graduations, and the day the local sports team wins a championship.

In bygone days, political offenders, military captives, and heretics were executed almost out of hand. There was but a thin pretense of justice in which the prisoner could confess (*shrive*) his sins to a priest and prepare his soul for death. Those who kept these unfortunate souls in thrall often allotted but a short time for confession, and this hurried procedure became known as *short shrift*. Nowadays, this compound means "to give scant attention, to make quick work of."

THE TRUE MEANINGS OF CHRISTMAS

The great English etymologist Owen Barfield once wrote, "Words may be made to disgorge the past that is bottled up inside of them, as coal and wine, when we kindle or drink them, yield up their bottled sunshine." When we uncap the sunshine that is stored inside the many words that relate to the Christmas season, we discover that the light that streams forth illuminates centuries of human history and customs.

The word *Christmas* derives from the Old English *Cristes Maesse,* meaning "the festival mass of Christ." *Christmas* is a fine example of a disguised compound, a word formed from two independent morphemes (meaning-bearing elements) that have become so closely welded together that their individual identities have been lost.

Turns out that the word *holiday* is another disguised compound, descending from the Old English *haligdaeg,* "holy day." With the change in pronunciation has come a change in meaning so that holidays, such as Independence Day and Labor Day, are not necessarily holy. The *day* in *holiday* has also been transmuted so that an American can enjoy a three-day holiday.

The name *Christ* is a translation of the Hebrew word *messiah,* "the anointed one," rendered through the Greek as Christós. *Jesus* also reaches back to the ancient Hebrew name Yeshua, one of the names for God.

114

We learn about Jesus through the *gospels*. *Gospel* is yet another disguised compound, from the Old English *god*, "good," and *spel*, "news." The gospels of Matthew, Mark, Luke, and John spread the good news of the life and work of Christ. No surprise then that the four men who wrote the gospels are called *evangelists*, from the Greek *euaggelion*, which also means "good news."

The babe was born in *Bethlehem*, a Hebrew word meaning "house of bread." The Christ child was laid in a *manger*, a word related to the French verb *manger*, "to eat." Why? Because Jesus's crib was a large wooden box that usually served as a trough for feeding cattle.

We call the worship of the newborn babe the *Adoration*, from the Latin *adoratio*: *ad-* "to," and *oro-* "pray"; hence, "to pray to." Among those who came to worship were wise men from the East, *magi*, a Latin word for "magician" or "astrologer." The number of wise men is never mentioned in the gospels; we infer three from the gifts bestowed on the Christ child.

The Greek letter *chi*, spelled with an *X*, is the first letter of the word *Xristos*, which is Greek for Christ. *Xmas*, then, is actually a Greek derivative that does not eradicate the name of Christ from *Christmas*. The name of the holiday has been abbreviated as *Xmas* for five hundred years. Slogans like "Put the Christ back in Christmas" were coined by people who don't know the history of *X*. No offense intended then or now by the *X*.

Yuletide as a synonym for the Christmas season dates back to a pagan and then Christian period of feasting about the time of the winter solstice, December 22. The origin of *Yule* is uncertain. One suggestion is that *Yule* comes from the Gothic *giul* or *hiul*, which meant "wheel." In this context, *Yule* signifies that the sun, like a wheel, has completed its annual journey. Whence the *tide* in *Yuletide?* From an Old English word meaning "time," as in *Eastertide.*

Christmas occurs shortly after the winter solstice, when the sun reaches its most southerly excursion relative to the celestial equator. The winter solstice enfolds the longest night of the year, just before the days slowly fill back up with brightness.

At the time of the summer and winter solstices, the sun, before journeying back toward the equator, appears to stand still. This phenomenon is reflected in the Latin roots of the word: *sol,* meaning "sun," and *sistere,* "to stand still."

Among the most fascinating Christmas etymologies are those for *Santa Claus* and *Kris Kringle.* When the Dutch came to the New World during the seventeenth century, the figure of Saint Nikolaas, their patron saint, was on the first ship. After the Dutch lost control of New Amsterdam, *Sinterklaas* (a form of *Saint Nikolaas*) became anglicized into *Santa Claus.*

Kris Kringle reflects an even more drastic change from one language to another. Immigrants from the Holy Roman Empire (now Germany, Austria, and Switzerland) settled in Pennsylvania in the seventeenth and eighteenth centuries. They held the custom that the Christ Child, "the Christ-kinkle," brought gifts for the children on Christmas Eve. When English-speaking settlers moved near these Pennsylvania Dutch (also known as Pennsylvania Deutsch), the Christ-kinkle became *Kris Kringle.* By the 1840s, Kris Kringle had irretrievably taken on the identity of St. Nicholas, or Santa Claus.

The word *carol* comes from the Greek word *choraulein,* "to accompany a chorus on a reed instrument." The word transmogrified to *carol* and came to signify a round dance. People originally performed carols on several occasions during the year. By the 1600s, carols involved singing only, and Christmas had become the main holiday for these songs.

Of the various plants associated with the Christmas season, the poinsettia possesses the most intriguing history etymologically. A Mexican legend tells of a penniless boy who presented to the Christ Child a beautiful plant with scarlet leaves that resembled the Star of Bethlehem. The Mexicans named the plant *Flor de la Noche Buena,* "Christmas Eve Flower." Dr. Joel Roberts Poinsett, the first U.S. minister to Mexico, came upon the red and green Christmas plant there in 1828 and brought it to the United States, where it was named in his honor in 1836. The poinsettia has become one of the most popular of Christmas plants—and one of the most misspelled words (*pointsettia, pointsetta, poinsetta*) in the English language.

Another botanical Christmas item is the pear tree. In the seasonal song "The Twelve Days of Christmas," have you ever wondered why the true love sends not only a partridge but also an entire pear tree? That's because in the early French version of the song the suitor gave only a partridge, which in French is rendered as *une pertriz.* A 1718 English version combined the two—"a partridge, *une pertriz*"—which, slightly corrupted, came out sounding like "a partridge in a pear tree." Ever since, the partridge has remained proudly perched in a pear tree.

A Merry Christ Mass and Happy Holy Days to all!

GEE WHIZ!

English speakers apparently take deeply to heart the biblical commandment not to use the Lord's name in vain and Christ's injunction to eschew all swearing, either by heaven or by earth.

We live in a culture in which calling out the name of Jesus Christ in church is a sign of moral rectitude. But, once outside, we have to find ways of not quite saying that name. Most prominent among those taboo euphemisms, as they are called, are *gee, geez,* and *gee whiz* (*Je-sus*). Add to that list *gee whillikers, geez Louise, jesum crow, Christmas, holy cow, holy crow, holy Christmas, cripes, criminey, crikey, by Jingo, by Jiminy, Jiminy Cricket, Jiminy Christmas, Judas Priest,* and even *jeepers creepers.*

These linguistic strategies have been labeled "taboo euphemisms" and "taboo deformations." Have you ever noticed how many different ways we've come up with to avoid saying *God* and *damnation?*: *gosh, golly, goodness gracious, good grief, good gravy, by gar, by golly, by gum, dad gum, doggone, gol dang, gol darn, dear me* (an approximation of the Italian *Dio mio,* "my God"), *jumpin' Jehoshaphat* ("jumping Jehovah"), *begorrah* (Irish for "by God"), *great Scott, gosh all fishhooks* ("God almighty"), *by gorey, by Godfrey,* W.C. Fields' *Godfrey Daniels, good gravy,* and *what in tarnation* ("damnation")!

More antique and elegant stratagems for skirting the name of the Almighty include *egad* ("ye gods"), *odds bodkins* (a shortening of "God's body"), *gadzooks* ("God's hooks," the nails of the cross), *drat* ("God rot"), *'sblood* ("God's blood"), and *zounds* ("God's wounds").

Who needs to shout, "Hell!" when Sam Hill (euphemism for "damn hell") is available to help us cuss *(curse)* in a socially acceptable manner? Sam Hill was not a particular person, but "Sam Hill" expressions, such as *what the Sam Hill!* and *mad as Sam Hill,* grew up in the American West in the 1830s. Sam Hill was a trusty friend of frontiersmen, especially when they needed to clean up their language in the presence of womenfolk. One can count among additional surrogates that flame up as *hell* the words *heck, hey, Halifax, Hoboken,* and *Jesse* ("if you don't watch out, you're going to catch Jesse").

☺ Name That Tune!

The word *bible* derives from the Greek *biblia*, which means "books." Indeed, the Bible is a whole library of books that contain many different kinds of literature—history, narrative, short stories, poetry, philosophy, riddles, fables, allegories, letters, and drama. Many parts of the Bible are highly dramatic because they show in detail the sweep of grand events as experienced by a vivid and diverse cast of persons.

In 2017, after fifty-six years representing the city where I live, the San Diego Chargers betrayed our trust and skulked away to Los Angeles. Instantly, the football team was dubbed the Los Angeles Judases. Most of us San Diego sports fans understood the biblical allusion because, reflecting the New Testament narrative about Judas Iscariot's betrayal of Jesus Christ, a traitorous man is now called a Judas.

As their hopes and fears, ambitions and tragedies, and laughter and sorrows unfold in the Bible, many of these men and women have become so familiar to so many readers that their names have become archetypal. Thus, a large man is a Goliath, an old man a Methuselah, a wise man a Solomon, an evil woman a Jezebel, a doer of good deeds a Good Samaritan, a long-suffering man a Job, a skeptical man a Doubting Thomas, a mighty hunter a Nimrod, and a strong man a Samson.

Here's a playlist of theme songs. Match each biblical personage with his or her appropriate popular song. *Examples:* Shadrach, Meshach, and Abednego's song would be "Great Balls of Fire!" owing to their placement into a fiery furnace by Nebuchadnezzar II in the Book of Daniel. Conversely, Eliphaz, Bildad, and Zophar's, who advised a blameless Job to repent, would be paired with "Cold Comfort."

1.	Absalom	"Blinded By the Light"
2.	Adam and Eve	"Coat of Many Colors"
3.	Bathsheba	"Crying Over You"
4.	Cain	"Do It Now, Do It Good"
5.	Daniel	"Hair"
6.	David	"I Could Have Danced All Night"
7.	Esther	"I Feel Pretty"
8.	The Good Samaritan	"I Got You Babe"
9.	Jezebel	"I'm Sorry"
10.	Job	"The Lady Is a Tramp"
11.	John the Baptist	"Let's Hear It For the Boy"
12.	Jonah	"The Lion Sleeps Tonight"
13.	Joseph	"Losing My Head Over You"
14.	Lazarus	"Psycho Killer"
15.	The Magi	"Raindrops Keep Fallin' On My Head"
16.	Mary Magdalene	"Rebel, Rebel"
17.	Methuselah	"The Second Time Around"
18.	Moses	"Shadow of a Doubt"
19.	Noah	"Starry Starry Night"
20.	Paul	"Stayin' Alive"
21.	Peter	"Strangers in Paradise"

22. Pharaoh's daughter	"The Wanderer"
23. Salome	"A Whale Of a Tale"
24. Samson	"Why's Everybody Always Picking on Me?"
25. Thomas	"Your Cheatin' Heart"

Answers

1. Absalom: "Rebel, Rebel" 2. Adam and Eve: "Strangers in Paradise" 3. Bathsheba: "Your Cheatin' Heart" 4. Cain: "Psycho Killer" 5. Daniel: "The Lion Sleeps Tonight"

6. David: "Let's Hear It For the Boy" 7. Esther: "I Feel Pretty" 8. The Good Samaritan: "Do It Now, Do It Good" 9. Jezebel: "The Lady is a Tramp" 10. Job: "Why's Everybody Always Picking on Me?"

11. John the Baptist: "Losing My Head Over You" 12. Jonah: "A Whale Of a Tale" 13. Joseph: "Coat of Many Colors" 14. Lazarus: "The Second Time Around" 15. The Magi: "Starry Starry Night"

16. Mary Magdalene: "Crying Over You" 17. Methuselah: "Stayin' Alive" 18. Moses: "The Wanderer" 19. Noah: "Raindrops Keep Fallin' On My Head" 20. Paul: "Blinded By the Light"

21. Peter: "I'm Sorry" 22. Pharaoh's daughter: "I Got You Babe" 23. Salome: "I Could Have Danced All Night" 24. Samson: "Hair" (could also be Absalom) 25. Thomas: "Shadow of a Doubt"

☺ BIBLE RIDDLES

R iddles are perhaps the most ancient of all verbal puzzles, dating back at least twenty-five hundred years. In the book of Judges, the mighty Samson comes upon a swarm of bees making honey in the carcass of a lion. From this, Samson makes a bet with the Philistines that they cannot solve his riddle: "Out of the eater came something to eat. Out of the strong came something sweet." After seven days of weeping, Samson's wife wheedles the answer out of him and conveys it to the Philistines. In a rage, Samson kills thirty of them and lays waste their city. Today we don't take riddles quite as seriously, but we do derive sweetness and strength from a cleverly turned poser.

Gaze upon modern riddles about four Old Testament personages—Adam and Eve, Noah, and Moses:

At what time of day was Adam created? *A little before Eve.*
Who was the champion runner of all time? *Adam. He was first in the human race.*
Why were Adam and Eve the happiest couple in history? *Because Eve couldn't tell Adam how many other men she could have married, and Adam couldn't tell Eve how much he loved his mother's cooking.*

Why were Adam and Eve kicked out of the Garden of Eden? *Because they were the first to ignore Apple terms & conditions.*

What excuse did Adam give to his children as to why they no longer lived in Eden? *"Your mother ate us out of house and home."*

What was the longest day in the Bible? *The one with no Eve.*

Did Eve ever have a date with Adam? *No, it was an apple.*

How were Adam and Eve prevented from gambling? *They lost their paradise.*

What did Adam and Eve never have but left to their children? *Belly buttons.*

What evidence is there that Adam and Eve were pretty noisy? *They raised Cain.*

When is meat first mentioned in the Bible? *When Noah took Ham onto the ark.*

Where did Noah keep the bees? *In the ark hives.*

Why couldn't people play cards on the ark? *Noah sat on the deck.*

Why couldn't Noah catch many fish? *He only had two worms.*

Who were the best financiers in the Bible? *Noah, who floated his stock while the whole world was in liquidation, and Pharaoh's daughter, who took a little prophet from the rushes on the banks.*

Who was the first man in the Bible to use a computer? *Moses. He downloaded data from the cloud to his tablet.*

How does Moses make his coffee? *Hebrews it.*

Who was the first man in the Bible to break all Ten Commandments? *Moses.*

How do we know for certain that Moses was a male? *He spent forty years wandering in the desert and never stopped to ask for directions.*

Who were the three most constipated men in the Bible? *Cain, because he wasn't Abel; Methuselah, who sat on the throne for nine-hundred years; and Moses, because God gave him two tablets and sent him into the wilderness.*

LOCATION, LOCATION

HAMBURG, GERMANY

HAMBURGER

FRANKFURT, GERMANY

FRANKFURTER

PUTTING WORDS
IN THEIR PLACES

Like the names of people, place names have similarly enriched the English language with many common words. An atlas of cities, towns, regions, and nations have become eponymously enshrined in our dictionaries, usually as uncapitalized nouns, verbs, or adjectives. We put words in their places and places in our words.

In order to spend more uninterrupted time at the gambling tables, John Montagu, Fourth Earl of Sandwich ("sand village"), ordered his servants to bring him an impromptu meal of slices of beef slapped between two slices of bread. Thus, America's favorite luncheon repast was rustled up to feed a nobleman's gambling addiction.

Somebody once defined a hamburger as "a humble immigrant hunk of meat that came to this country from Germany and soared to fame on a bun." That somebody was perfectly right. In its native land the dish was originally called "Hamburg steak," taking its name from the West German city of Hamburg.

After the Hamburg steak arrived in the United States midway through the last century with the first great wave of German immigrants, its name began to change. Ultimately the Hamburg steak dropped its capital *H*, acquired the suffix -*er*, lost the *steak*, and moved from the platter to the plane between two slices of baked dough. Voila: a hamburger!

The adventure in word evolution didn't stop there. Somewhere along the way, speakers of English liberally interpreted *burger* to mean "sandwich made with a bun." Once *burger* became a new word part, *cheeseburger, beefburger, baconburger, fishburger, chiliburger,* and a tray full of other burgers entered the American scene and gullet. *Frankfurter,* which takes its name from Frankfurt, Germany, has traveled the same linguistic road. *Furter* is now used to denote almost any kind of sandwich with protein slapped inside an elongated bun, as in *chickenfurter* and *fishfurter.*

And speaking of frankfurters, do you know that Charlemagne mustered his Franks and set out with great relish to assault and pepper his enemies, but he couldn't ketchup? Frankly, I never sausage a pun. It's the wurst!

These yummy sandwiches only begin to illustrate the place that places have in our language:

A *bikini* is a skimpy, two-piece swimsuit named after the Bikini atoll in the Pacific Marshall Islands, on which atomic bombs were tested—a truly explosive and figurative word. During the COVID-19 apocalypse, a matching medical mask and bikini top and bottom were dubbed a *trikini.*

The *limerick,* the most popular of all humorous verse forms in English, hails from a county in Ireland. One theory says that Irish mercenaries used to compose verses in that form about each other and then join in a chorus of "When we get back to Limerick town, 'twill be a glorious morning."

Blarney, which means "smooth-sounding flattery," derives from the name of a town and castle in County Cork, Ireland. An inscription on the wall of the castle proclaims that anyone brave enough to scale the wall and kiss a particular stone will be rewarded with the gift of influencing others through cajolery.

Two-and-a-half millennia ago, a little band of ten thousand Athenians defeated a host of one hundred thousand Persians at the battle of Marathon. Pheidippides, a courageous runner, brought the news of the glorious victory to Athens, which lay twenty-six miles away. He exclaimed, "Joy to you! We've won!" and died from the exertion of his immense journey. Pheidippides' heroism has inspired the *marathon,* a modern-day road race.

Nineteenth-century sailors were sometimes drugged and then forced into service on ships plying the unpopular route from San Francisco to China. From Shanghai, the name of that Chinese port we get the verb *to shanghai,* "to secure someone's services through force."

Bedlam, a contraction of "St. Mary's of Bethlehem," a sixteenth-century London hospital for the insane, has become a word for uproar or confusion.

Donnybrook, another word for disorder, in this case a wild brawl, comes down to us from the name of a fair, held in, Donnybrook, an Irish town near Dublin, infamous for its fist fights and rowdy behavior.

As an alternative to cumbersome tails on a formal full-dress dinner coat, the *tuxedo,* a tailless dinner coat, originated in Tuxedo Junction, an exclusive community about forty miles north of New York City. This short evening coat was an immediate sensation during the Gay Nineties; it is still obligatory at many formal functions.

The Pilgrims found in America a wild fowl somewhat similar in appearance to a fowl they had known back in England—a bird that had acquired the name *turkey* because it was first imported by way of Turkey, a Middle Eastern nation that doesn't celebrate Thanksgiving or football. Because we perceive this bird as ugly in appearance and voice, we sometimes assign its name to people we don't care for.

The inhabitants of the ancient Greek district Laconia were noted for their ability to say a lot in a few words. During a siege of their capital, a Roman general sent a note to this city's commander warning that if the Romans captured the city, they would burn it to the ground. From within the city gates came back the terse reply: "If!" The city's name lives on in the adjective *laconic*, "marked by spare speech." Sparta, a town in the district of Laconia, bequeaths us the adjective *Spartan,* "marked by strict self-discipline."

Many years ago, cloth was imported into England from Silesea, then part of Germany. The material was of such poor quality that the English referred to it contemptuously as "that cloth from Silesea," or "Silesea cloth." Ultimately the phrase was shortened even further to "sleazy cloth," and that's how *sleazy* was fabricated as a popular adjective for "cheap and shoddy." Recently the word spawned such offspring as *sleaze, sleazebag,* and *sleazeball.*

In 1516, British Lord Chancellor Sir Thomas More published *Utopia,* in which life on the island of Utopia is socially and economically ideal. The Greek etymons embedded in *Utopia* are *ou*, "not, no"; *eu*, "good," as in *eulogy* and *euphemism*; and *topos*, "place," which coalesce into "a good place that doesn't exist."

Another place name born at the tip of a pen is *Serendip*, a form of the old Arabic name for the island of Ceylon. Horace Walpole coined the word *serendipity* in his story "The Three Princes of Serendip," the heroes in which "were always making discoveries, by accident or sagacity, of things they were not in quest of." *Serendipity* is the ability to make lucky finds by accident. Many people use the word to describe any stroke of luck.

Our Native American Heritage

More than four centuries ago, the roots of Thanksgiving first took hold in our American soil. We living today commemorate the solemn dinner, back in the fall of 1621, shared by the Pilgrims of Plymouth, Massachusetts, and the Wampanoag ("Dawnlanders") Indians, the local tribe who generously pulled the fragile Pilgrim colony through their first winter and taught them how to plant corn.

Let's talk turkey about our indigenous, Native American heritage. Suppose you had been one of the early explorers or settlers of North America. You would have found many things in your new land unknown to you. The handiest way of filling voids in your vocabulary would have been to ask the locals what words they used. The early colonists began borrowing words from friendly Native Americans almost from the moment of their first contact, and many of those names have remained in our everyday language:

In a letter that British explorer John Smith wrote home in 1608, he described a critter that the Virginia Algonquians (Powhatan) called a *rahaughcum* or an *aroughcan*, "he scratches with his hands." Over the years the word was shortened and simplified to *raccoon*, one of the very first English words coined in America.

Pronouncing many of the Native American words was difficult for the early explorers and settlers. In many instances, they had to shorten and simplify the names. Identify the following animals from their Native American names:

apossoum (Don't play dead now.)
otchig (How much wood?)
segankw (What's black and white and stinks all over?)

The hidden animals are: *opossum* (Powhatan Algonquian), *woodchuck* (from Ojibwa Algonquian for a weasel-like fisher), and *skunk* (Abenaki Algonquian). To this menagerie we may add the likes of *caribou* (Micmac), *chipmunk* (Ojibwa), *moose* (Abenaki), and *muskrat* (Massachusett *musquash*).

You can expand the lexicon with the likes of food—*squash* (Narragansett), *pecan* (Ojibwa), *hominy* (Virginia Algonquian), *pone* (Delaware Algonquian), *pemmican* (Cree), and *succotash* (Narragansett)—and other ingredients of Native American life: *moccasin* (Narragansett), *toboggan* (Micmac Algonquian), *tomahawk* (Virginia Algonquian), *wigwam* (Abenaki), *teepee* (Dakota Siouan), *caucus* (Virginia Algonquian), *powwow* (Narragansett), *wampum* (Narragansett), *bayou* (Choctaw Muskogean), *potlatch* (Nootka), *hogan* (Navajo Athabascan), *hickory* (Virginia Algonquian), *kayak* (Inuit), *parka* (Aleut), *totem* (Ojibwa), *sachem* (Narragansett), *squaw* (Massachusett), *papoose* (Narragansett), and *mugwump* (Massachusett).

If you examine a map of the United States, you will realize how freely settlers used words of Indian origin to name the places where we live. Rivers, lakes, ponds, creeks, mountains, valleys, counties, towns, and cities as large as Chicago (from a Fox word that means "place that stinks of wild onions") bear Native American names. Four of our five Great

Lakes—Huron, Ontario, Michigan, and Erie—and twenty-five of our states have names borrowed from Native American words:

Alabama: name of a tribe in the Creek Confederacy, meaning "plant cutters"; *Alaska:* "mainland" (Aleut); *Arizona:* "having a little spring" (Pima); *Arkansas:* named for the Siouan Kansa tribe (Dhegiha Siouan); *Connecticut:* "place of the long tidal river" (Southern New England Algonquian);

Idaho: "enemy" (Kiowa-Apache Athabascan); *Illinois:* "he speaks the typical way" (Ottawa from Miami-Illinois); *Iowa:* "sleepy ones" (Santee Siouan); *Kansas:* named for the Siouan Kansa tribe (Dhegiha Siouan); *Kentucky:* "meadowland" (Wyandot Iroquoian);

Massachusetts: "great hillock place" (Massachusett); *Michigan:* "great water (Ojibwa); *Minnesota:* "milky blue river" (Dakota); *Mississippi:* "large river" (Ottawa); *Missouri:* "wood boat, dugout" (Miami-Illinois);

Nebraska: "flat water" (Omaha Siouan); *North Dakota* and *South Dakota:* "friendly"; "allies" (Dakota Siouan); *Ohio:* "great river" (Seneca Iroquoian); *Oklahoma:* "red people" (Choctaw);

Tennessee: "name of a Cherokee village"; *Texas:* "friends, allies" (Caddo); *Utah:* named after the tribe Ute, "high" (Western Apache); *Wisconsin:* "It lies red," referring to the Wisconsin River (Miami-Illinois); *Wyoming:* "at the big river flat" (Munsee).

Some of our loveliest place names began life as Native American words—*Susquehanna* (Algonquian), *Shenandoah* (Oneida), and *Rappahannock* (Delaware). Such names are the stuff of poetry. To the poet Walt Whitman, *Monongahela*

(Unami Delaware) "rolls with venison richness upon the palate." About the Lenape Indians William Penn wrote: "I know not a language spoken in Europe that hath words of more sweetness and greatness." How fortunate we are that the poetry the First Peoples heard in the American landscape lives on in our American language.

☺PUNS THAT BABYLON

I'm a member of the Flat Earth Society. We have chapters around the globe. I'm also a member of the Round Earth Society. Our chapters extend to the four corners of the Earth

We hear a lot these days about geographical illiteracy, the inability of Americans to name the capital of their state or to locate Afghanistan or even the Pacific Ocean on a world map. As an antidote to such spatial ignorance, here's a chance for you to increase your geographical knowledge as well as your skill in fabricating outrageous puns.

Complete each statement below with the name of a country or republic in the list that follows. Each item appears just once in the answers at the end of the game. *Example:* Wear your winter coat today, or you'll get <u>Chile</u>. *Another example:* I hope you'll enjoy playing this punderful game and won't <u>Crimea</u> river about it.

Belgium	Denmark	Greece
Bolivia	Egypt	Haiti
Brazil	Egypt	Holland
China	France	Hungary
Cuba	Germany	India

Iran	Panama	Sudan
Iraq	Peru	Sweden
Israel	Poland	Syria
Jamaica	Rumania	Tibet
Kenya	Russia	Turkey
Laos	Saudi	Ukraine
Norway	Senegal	Uruguay
Pakistan	Spain	Wales

1. I'm not kidding. I'm _____s.
2. You stood still, but _____.
3. I'm between _____ and a hard place.
4. Save the _____ before they become extinct.
5. I don't _____ broke my expensive _____ vase.

6. I'll _____ board in two.
7. Alco_____ cigarettes are bad habits.
8. Don't put the chair in the study, Mark. Put it in the _____.
9. Give me a good _____ I'll be willing _____ that I can vault fifteen feet.
10. Little Miss Muffet liked neither curds _____.

11. Your leather wallet is fake, but mine _____.
12. Your backpack is brown, but my back_____.
13. Your zebra is healthy, but my ze_____.
14. A strong antibody will defeat a _____ time.
15. I'm a gal, and _____, and you've never _____ like me.

16. I see your daughter is taking piano lessons. _____ do it?
17. As soil erosion increases, we keep los_____.
18. I love coffee, but I _____. Please give me a _____ sugar to _____ my coffee.
19. That rotten _____. _____ me.
20. Dan's car plowed into mine, so I'm going to _____.

21. On Thanksgiving I get _____ for _____, if it doesn't have too much _____.
22. If you are obsessed with kangaroos, you have kanga_____.
23. I can't figure out what's causing thi_____ in my elbow.
24. If _____ your neck, you'll be able to see over the fence.
25. The sun will come up when it comes up. You can't _____ sunrise.

26. You've been acting crazy. I wonder what's gotten _____.
27. If you can pan a pa, I can _____.
28. With _____ like these, who needs enemies?
29. Please be quiet so that I can _____se this book.
30. Hey, Jim. _____ please ring the _____?

Answers

1. Syria 2. Iran 3. Iraq 4. Wales 5. Bolivia / China
6. Saudi 7. Holland 8. Denmark 9. Poland / Tibet
10. Norway

11. Israel 12. Pakistan 13. Brazil 14. Germany 15. Uruguay /
Senegal

16. Jamaica 17. England 18. Haiti / Cuba / Sweden
19. Laos / Egypt 20. Sudan

21. Hungary / Turkey / Greece 22. Romania 23. Spain
24. Ukraine 25. Russia

26. India 27. Panama 28. France 29. Peru 30. Kenya /
Belgium

ACKNOWLEDGMENTS

I am grateful for permission to adapt in *So That's What It Means!* some items that have appeared in my Pocket Books, Gibbs Smith, and Marion Street Press books. Thousands of thanks to Eileen and Charlie Patton for their loving labors to make this book the very best it could be.

Art credits: covers and Teddy Bear, by Todd Smith; clouds by Novoklimov, commons license; moon image from George Méliès, *Le Voyage dans la Lune* (1902); Adam and Eve, by Albrecht Dürer, 1504; Hamburg, by Aliasdoobs, commons license; Frankfurt, by Markus Schüller, commons license.

AUTHOR BIOGRAPHY

R ichard Lederer is the author of more than fifty books about language, history, and humor, including his best-selling *Anguished English* series and his current books, *A Treasury of Halloween Humor, A Treasury of Christmas Humor, Richard Lederer's Ultimate Book of Literary Trivia,* and *A Pleasury of Word & Phrase Origins.* He is a founding co-host of *A Way With Words,* broadcast on Public Radio.

Dr. Lederer's column, *Lederer on Language,* appears in newspapers and magazines throughout the United States. He has been named International Punster of the Year and Toastmasters International's Golden Gavel winner.

He lives in San Diego with his wife, Simone van Egeren.

richardhlederer@gmail.com
www.verbivore.com

Made in USA - Crawfordsville, IN
78815_9781956503029
05.06.2022 1954